creative ESSENTIALS

Dan Williams

WEB TV SERIES
how to make and market them

creative ESSENTIALS

To Anne

First published in 2012 by Kamera Books
an imprint of Oldcastle Books,
PO Box 394, Harpenden, Herts, AL5 1XJ
www.kamerabooks.com

A CIP catalogue record for this book is available from the British Library.

978-1-84243-785-8 (Print)
978-1-84243-786-5 (epub)
978-1-84243-787-2 (kindle)
978-1-84243-788-9 (pdf)

Typeset by Elsa Mathern in Franklin Gothic 9 pt
Printed and bound by CPI Group (UK) Ltd, Croydon, CRO 4YY

MIX
Paper from
responsible sources
FSC® C013604

ACKNOWLEDGEMENTS

Thank you to all of the talented and innovative web series professionals whom I contacted while researching this book. The new media community is extremely supportive and I am always grateful for their insight.

Thank you to Hannah Patterson, Anne Hudson, and the wonderful Kamera Books team for their helpful notes and tremendous support.

And thank you to my wife for her constant inspiration.

CONTENTS

Preface 9

1.   INTRODUCTION TO WEB TV SERIES 11
2.   DEFINING SUCCESS 19
3.   DEVELOPING THE IDEA 33
4.   FINANCING THE PROJECT 57
5.   CREATING A MARKETING PLAN 69
6.   PRE-PRODUCTION 83
7.   PRODUCTION 95
8.   POST-PRODUCTION 109
9.   DISTRIBUTION 119
10.   SUSTAINABILITY 137
11.   TRADITIONAL MEDIA OPPORTUNITIES 149
12.   INDUSTRY INTERVIEWS 159
13.   RECOMMENDED WEB SERIES 183

      Appendix: Two Episodes of *Asylum* Script 189
      Endnotes 216
      Index 222

PREFACE

This is an entertainment medium without a lot of history or precedent. As soon as one path to success is established, it quickly becomes obsolete and is replaced by additional innovations in the marketplace.

How do you create a hit web series? The truth is that what works for one show is not replicable by another.

After helping a friend of mine who wrote and directed a web series, the idea crept into my head that I should create my own show as well. Producing *Asylum* gave me the opportunity to dive head-first into web TV. I was new to the game, and struggled to find any reliable how-to guides or best-practices.

So I talked to as many people working in new media as I could. I wanted to find out what worked for them, and what did not. What steps they took to reach their goals. And what mistakes they made. I attended panel discussions and networking events, and read every article I could about new shows and industry announcements.

This book is a collection of the information I gathered while producing content and exploring the new media space. It contains market research, breakdowns of the latest trends and technology, and web-specific tools for both aspiring and experienced filmmakers. There are also personal anecdotes from people working in new media from a variety of backgrounds.

1. INTRODUCTION TO WEB TV SERIES

When I started this book, I wanted to write something that presented all the options, scenarios, and possible routes one could take while developing their own web series. Simply put: I wanted to create the kind of resource I wish I'd had before making my own show.

As internet connections become faster, it is only getting easier to stream videos online. The vast majority of internet users watch video content, and the average amount viewed continues to increase as well.[1] Production costs, meanwhile, are decreasing as high-end cameras and editing software become more available to consumers. Websites like YouTube allow users from all over the world to upload and share their own creations.

You have surely noticed these trends yourself. Odds are that you have watched plenty of content – perhaps you have even posted a few videos of your own. What is important to note is that, out of this new web-based production and distribution model, a new medium of entertainment has emerged. Somewhere along the path of making original online videos, content creators began crafting *serialised* programmes.

These creators posted new content on a consistent basis and built an audience of regular viewers. Successful web videos no longer relied solely on a one-shot upload 'going viral' to become a hit. Whether they were flash cartoons like *Homestar Runner*, fictionalised blogs like *lonelygirl15*, machinima animation[2] like *Red vs Blue*, or sketches like the YouTube duo *Smosh* – a new trend developed in online video.

Creators promised new material on a specific schedule and focused on building a community of fans around their videos' brand.

The only thing more contested than the exact genesis of the medium is its name. Early adopters tended toward *web television*. But what is 'television' if it is not being watched on a TV? These new online programmes are broken into episodes and feel relatively like abbreviated versions of traditional television shows. However, many of them feature subject matter, use production techniques, and are uniquely structured in ways that differ greatly from their TV equivalents. Watching 'web television' is a very different viewing experience than simply watching a TV show on your computer.

Many have now taken to calling these serialised online videos *web TV series* or simply *web series*. The medium is one that took off in a hurry and has begun to capture the public's attention – as well as the attention of advertisers and studios. Web series have given voices to those left out of traditional entertainment and provided new opportunities for independent artists.

A CASE STUDY (WITH BACON)

Montreal natives Harley Morenstein and Sterling Toth started by recording something they loved to do: eating greasy food. In October 2010, the pair teamed up with some friends to create a pizza made out of all the fast food they could gather – burgers, chicken nuggets, tacos, French fries, and onion rings. Then they ate it and posted the footage on YouTube.[3]

When the video's view count soared past the 100,000 mark, Morenstein and Toth decided to produce more content. Their series, dubbed *Epic Meal Time*, releases new videos every Tuesday. With an over-the-top style and aggressive attitude toward food consumption, the duo lead the creation of ridiculously high-calorie feasts (which usually include layers upon layers of bacon).

In three months, the series accumulated over three million views. Currently, their total views are over 300 million. They built an audience of people who enjoyed their *Jackass*-like sensibilities and perhaps wanted to binge vicariously through the show. Their YouTube channel became the fastest to reach one million subscribers, completing the task in under nine months. Morenstein and Toth monetise their series through advertising on YouTube, merchandise sales on their website, and referral programs.

The creators of *Epic Meal Time* are now represented by the Gersh Agency and managed by Brillstein Entertainment Partners. They have been featured in *Entertainment Weekly* and were guests on *The Tonight Show with Jay Leno*. Morenstein and Toth recently closed a deal to develop their concept as a television pilot for the G4 network.[4]

A CASE STUDY (WITH UCB)

Upright Citizens Brigade alums Abbi Jacobson and Ilana Glazer have produced two seasons of a sometimes-scripted, sometimes-improvised comedy called *Broad City*. In the show, Jacobson and Glazer play exaggerated versions of themselves – confused and insecure as they navigate life in New York.[5] The series is every bit as awkward and funny as its lead actresses and reflects their distinct point of view (which the creators describe as empowering to women, without having a big message).[6]

Since early 2010, the duo has achieved cult status online. Their videos do not have nearly the amount of views as *Epic Meal Time*, but the series has been mentioned in *Huffington Post*, *Time Out New York* and the *Late Night with Jimmy Fallon* blog. Jacobson and Glazer have honed their style and sensibilities with the show, and push themselves creatively – for example, one episode paid homage to Spike Lee's *Do the Right Thing*, including a choreographed dance routine.

The unique nature of *Broad City* caught the eye of UCB co-founder Amy Poehler (*Parks and Recreation*), who helped bring the series to FX. Poehler will executive produce a half-hour pilot that Jacobson and Glazer are writing for the network.[7]

WHY WEB SERIES?

So, why do filmmakers choose to make a web series in the first place? Or, more than that, why do some creators *prefer* the online medium over others? There are several elements that make producing web series projects different to, say, a short film or television show.

Worldwide distribution

Distributing a show online allows your project to easily reach audiences all over the world. Not long ago, the model for independent filmmakers relied on festivals and art house theatres to exhibit their work. Worldwide distribution was only possible if a larger company acquired the film.

Posting a video to YouTube or other hosting site immediately makes it available to viewers across the globe. There is virtually no limit to the potential reach of your project. Of course, self-distribution like this also puts the pressure of marketing on your shoulders as well. You have the resources, but also the responsibility of attracting the audience you want.

Engaging viewers

On the web, you have the opportunity to engage your viewers for feedback and support. Instantly after watching, your audience can leave comments about your project. They can communicate via Facebook or Twitter, and share their thoughts. As a filmmaker, this gives you the chance to solicit reactions to your series, figure out what worked and what did not, and hopefully grow as a writer, producer, director, or actor.

Fans can also chat with each other about their favourite shows. Social media gives you the ability to help cultivate a community of viewers around your show. You can speak to them directly, provide updates about your project, and give your audience a look at the creative process behind the show.

Serialised storytelling

Telling stories or establishing a format over several consecutive episodes allows web series creators the opportunity to continuously perfect their projects. For scripted series, serialised shows allow writers to expand their stories beyond a single short or feature film. Actors have the chance for more in-depth character exploration. Hosts of non-scripted formats can develop episode segments that maximise audience engagement.

Monetisation opportunities

New ad revenue sharing models, brand-sponsored content, and an investment by large studios in online-specific content have provided incentives for filmmakers to create web video content.[8] The medium will continue to feature one-person video blogs and plenty of cat footage, but the space is increasingly becoming populated by talented professionals. Web series are a great place for experimentation and side projects; they are also how many filmmakers earn a living.

Independent producers can partner with established online networks or distribute themselves. Videos can feature ads or product placement. Web series creators can sell merchandise or ask for donations from fans. There are a number of creative ways for filmmakers to continue telling their stories and eventually make money doing what they love.

THERE ARE NO RULES

Creating a web series provides filmmakers with a tremendous amount of autonomy. You are your own boss, which means that you are in charge of every aspect of your art – from development to execution, distribution to marketing. Because of this, responsibility rests solely with you to make your show a success.

So, what makes a good web series? The two shows highlighted as case studies in this chapter seemingly could not be more different. From their subject matter to execution, each had their own methods of production. Yet each connected with an audience and helped their creators find new opportunities online.

Whether you are a writer, director or actor, producing a show by yourself or collaborating with others, this book will discuss all of the tasks that web series creators perform in order to make a successful show. The book draws upon personal experiences producing web series, making mistakes and learning along the way. It also draws upon knowledge from friends, colleagues and leaders in the new media industry.

Web series is an evolving, ever-changing medium. It is a young industry with few templates and even fewer rules. Working in the space can therefore be a trial by fire at times. Hopefully this book will provide insights and examples into all aspects of web series creation, and give you the tools necessary to reach your goals. You can read about, and learn from, the experiences of others. Then you will be able to make something uniquely your own.

INTERVIEW WITH JEAN MICHEL ALBERT

Jean Michel Albert is the founder and president of the Marseille Web Fest. For the first year of the festival in 2011, web series writers, producers, directors and actors from around the world were invited to exhibit their projects. Shows from countries such as France, Italy, Spain, Israel, India, Canada, the US and the UK were all represented. Attendees were able to meet with international exhibitors, transmedia developers and other experts in the industry. Jean Michel has watched the medium grow tremendously in recent years, and sees a world of opportunity for new web series creators.

What inspired you to create a festival exclusively for web series?

As a producer of web series, I egotistically thought, 'If there is no one to critique the artistic quality of TV series or movies in movie theatres, who is going to pose the aesthetic question regarding web series? One can imagine all, or almost all, their economic models, their hope in the number of viewers they can reach, but who really worries about their content? Where is the critical discourse to cover the potential creative explosion of this new type of production?'

It therefore seemed imperative for me to create a European festival so as to have a clearer understanding of the hundreds of web series which are created every year. The only well-known festival is in Los Angeles. Therefore I flew to the US and came to LAWEBFEST, organised by Michael Ajakwe. This was a real shock for me. First the joy of meeting the founder of the festival, but especially the shock of meeting so much talent from around the world. I had no doubt as to what to do when I left. I came back to France and organised the Marseille Web Fest, which was a real success.

What surprised you about the quality and content of the projects submitted to the festival?

We watched 130 web series, and retained 22. It is evident that only the best on an artistic basis were retained. But, overall, I was surprised by the level of quality of all candidates. Whatever the country of origin, the majority of the web series were really very interesting, well written, played by very good actors. I think this comes from the fact that a web series has much more of a chance to be seen by [an international audience] than a classic TV series. The writers will tend to act as real professionals as the critique is more cutting on social networks. Just watch YouTube, for instance. They can be very tough on those who put videos on the web.

We had some pretty intense discussions with the members of the selection committee. It was really difficult to choose the 22 web series as winners of the competition.

What future international opportunities do you foresee for web series creators?

On a professional and human level, I'd say that it gives them the opportunity to show their work to professionals, prove to the industry that they have the necessary talent to do a long production, or be entrusted with the creation of a series on TV. Ten years ago, it was very difficult for a writer, producer, or even an unknown actor to get [attention]. Unless you're lucky enough to know the head of a studio, or make a short film at the end of a university year and attend all festivals and get a prize, it is Mission Impossible. The internet has allowed an extraordinary visibility. Many talents, especially in the USA, have been recognised thanks to the internet.

On an economic level, I believe that certain web series can compete with any TV shows in the world. In addition, the scarcity of good programmes and the multiplicity of channels force the owners of these same channels to acquire this type of programme, or else see their viewers dwindle. It is the case in the US where many web series have become cult series on TV. In France and in Europe, more and more TV channels are interested in web series because of the number of viewers who go on the net. These TV channels no longer hesitate to produce web series and to show them on TV.

In any case, the better the quality of the web series, the better the chance of finding producers and making money!

2. DEFINING SUCCESS

New York-based actor Al Thompson enjoyed success early in his career with supporting roles in films such as *The Royal Tenenbaums* and *A Walk to Remember*. But the enterprising Thompson was not completely satisfied with his opportunities; indeed, he was often frustrated by the lack of them. So, using his own money and calling in a few favours (having friends in film school with access to equipment is always helpful), he created and starred in a web comedy called *Johnny B Homeless*, based upon his experiences couch-crashing when he first moved to Hollywood.

The witty and well-produced series was voted Audience Choice at the New York Television Festival in 2009 and caught the attention of Atom.com. The Comedy Central-controlled hosting site acquired the show for exclusive distribution the following year.

Since then, Al Thompson has been one of the hardest-working talents in new media. He is founder and CEO of his own production company, ValDean Entertainment. Thompson continues to write, produce, and star in original web shows. Recently, his drama *Lenox Avenue* and sci-fi series *Odessa* have been acquired by BET for online distribution. New media is a medium for entrepreneurial filmmakers, and Al Thompson is a great example of that spirit.

Web series creators have the opportunity to control all facets of their show – from development and production, to marketing and distribution. In some respects, creating a web series is similar to starting a business. And, as any MBA knows, you do not start a business without a plan.

Every day there is a new series being uploaded to the web.[9] Many of these only last a few episodes before their websites go dark. But a handful of these series go on to become YouTube partners, strike sponsorship deals to finance more episodes, or even develop into television shows. What separates these projects from others is planning for success, and understanding what it takes to be successful.

The specific tools necessary to achieve your goals vary depending on what kind of web series you create. Therefore, by first identifying the objectives of your show, you can make informed decisions about acquiring the resources needed to execute your vision. You can also study other shows with similar aspirations in order to craft your plan.

It is time for you to ask the question: what do you want to do with your show?

HAVE FUN

While you may not have purchased this book to help you post strictly recreational videos online, it is important to remember that all these new media tools can be used to simply have a little fun. Instead of merely griping about how much garbage is on television,[10] you have the ability to program your own networks online. And without any executives to report to, you have the opportunity to be as creative as you like.

Write your own theme songs. Design your own opening title graphics. Experiment with storytelling formats. Be outrageous. Be bold. If your objective is only to enjoy the process, then let that be your definition of success. Do not worry about view counts or marketing strategy. If you stumble upon a viral hit, then you can reevaluate your goals.

But do not break the bank on these types of projects. Your show should be produced using equipment you already own (or can borrow), require virtually no financial investment, and be made in your spare time.

MAKE THIS YOUR FULL-TIME JOB

In 2010, the top ten YouTube partners – that is, channels whose content was deemed appropriate for special advertising partnerships – each earned over $100,000. Hosting site Blip (blip.tv) reports that some of their producers earned as much as $500,000 in ad revenue. There is certainly money to be made for web series creators. But this is not the lottery (unless, perhaps, you are Rebecca Black). Earning an income equal to a full-time job requires a full-time commitment.

In order for a show to earn a significant amount of ad revenue, it needs to generate total views in the millions.[11] Therefore, the most successful YouTubers and web series programmers post new content nearly every day. This high level of output requires creators, at least initially, to keep production costs very low. Most use equipment that they already own, which eliminates rental fees and gives them the ability to shoot on short notice. They also use convenient, mostly free locations such as homes, cars, or outdoor spaces, or green-screen rigs that they build themselves. Many creators are also the stars of their shows, or feature friends willing to appear for free.

Case study

This book will go into greater detail later about becoming a YouTube partner or making ad revenue-sharing deals with other distributors. To give you a better idea of what types of shows find sustainability and success through this method, though, let us take a quick look at YouTube aficionados Freddie Wong and Brandon Laatsch.

The videos posted on the freddiew YouTube channel usually star Freddie and feature fun, creative, and astonishingly professional-grade special effects that Brandon renders himself. Episode concepts tend to focus on video-game characters and scenarios integrating with everyday life. They are relatively short, simply structured skits that highlight the filmmakers' ability to craft their own unique CGI environments.

Since launching the channel in 2005, Freddie has engaged his fans at every opportunity. Most videos end with links to behind-the-scenes featurettes and recorded responses to viewer comments. Freddie and his team also organised a cross-country road trip to meet some of their fans, as well as shooting new videos at interesting fan-submitted locations.

Only after years of producing original, high-quality videos and becoming a YouTube partner was the freddiew team able to leave their other jobs to work on their web series full-time in 2010. They worked hard doing something they enjoy, and now have the seventh most subscribed-to channel on YouTube.

Other examples

Because YouTube success depends largely upon posting videos on a near-daily basis, many creators star in their own videos and produce using the video-blog format. Justine Ezarik (ijustine), Philip DeFranco (sxephil) and Ray William Johnson are typical examples, as well as the Fred character created by Lucas Cruikshank. Sketch comedy also lends itself to YouTube popularity (for example, the channel TotallySketch). Shows with simple formats, such as TheFineBros' *Kids React* (in which children watch and comment on the latest quirky web videos), can also find YouTube success.

Some web series are more ambitious in their quality, which, of course, leads to higher production costs and the need for upfront financing in order to maintain sustainability. Content creators of this kind solicit corporate sponsorships and exclusive distribution deals in order to meet their goals. These shows, like the YouTube programmers above, need to demonstrate the ability to reach a significant amount of viewers. However, they need not reach super-high view counts or post a large volume of material, so long as they target a specific demographic and build a community of fans.

Case studies

In 2007, actress Felicia Day drew upon her gaming experiences to create and produce three episodes of a web series called *The Guild*, which chronicles the online and offline lives of internet gamers. After posting the show on YouTube, Felicia's enthusiastic audience helped her finance two more episodes of the series. She had successfully identified a niche of dedicated and active fans.

Because of the show's professional production values, the strong identity of its viewers, and the subject matter of the show, Felicia was able to make a sponsorship deal with Microsoft to finance future seasons of her series. Through the deal, the show now premieres via various Microsoft platforms, such as Xbox Live, which fits in with the show's targeted demographic. *The Guild* has been running for five seasons, and even spawned its own comic-book series.

Alternatively, sponsors can be brought onto a project early in the development process so that they can further be integrated into the show's storytelling. Actress and producer Illeana Douglas caught the attention of mega-brand IKEA with a YouTube series that she produced called *Supermarket of the Stars*. The furniture company liked the concept so much that they collaborated with Illeana to develop a new show set inside one of the company's stores. The series, *Easy to Assemble*, launched in 2008 and is currently in its third season.

Other examples

There are also opportunities for web series creators to continue producing their shows via exclusive distribution partnerships. For example, Syfy.com has picked up the Canadian-produced steampunk adventure *Riese* and the retro sci-fi serial *Mercury Men*. Some series, such as the teenage drama *Anyone But Me* (which is concluding after three critically acclaimed seasons), are able to maintain independent sustainability through a combination of crowd-sourcing, ad revenue, and DVD/merchandise sales.

CREATE A PORTFOLIO PIECE

Aspiring filmmakers are always searching for ways to break into the industry. What better way to showcase your abilities as a writer, producer, director or actress than creating a mini-TV show? Without the burden of reporting to any network executives, you have the ability to demonstrate your unique creative voice. And if you would like to use your project only as a portfolio piece, sustainability does not necessarily need to factor into your development process.

As with the short film format, there are a number of high-profile festivals in which new media projects can compete. In addition to this exposure, the web also provides the opportunity for executives, producers, agents and managers to find your work organically, increasing your potential of being discovered.

As established studios, television networks and large brands begin to produce more original web content, there will increasingly be more opportunities for filmmakers with experience in the space. Emerging YouTube talents, for example, are partnering with production companies to expand their brands. They are hiring directors, writers and producers – just like any traditional media project would.

Case study

North Carolina natives, friends and filmmakers Rhett McLaughlin and Link Neal began posting original videos to the web in 2006. Their songs, sketches and video blogs built a steady fan base; the duo's YouTube channel RhettandLink currently has received over 100 million total views. One of their most popular videos is an elaborate stop-motion skit called *T-SHIRT WAR!!*, which they made in conjunction with fellow YouTubers Joe Penna (mysteryguitarman) and Billy Reid (verytasteful). The video's creativity and unique style caught the attention of McDonald's and Coca-Cola, who employed the team to create a commercial using the same concept.

Rhett and Link continued to partner with companies and produce branded online videos. One of these projects was the MicroBilt sponsored series *iLoveLocalCommercials*, which featured the duo creating free commercials for local businesses submitted by users. The show was such a success that IFC developed the idea for television. *Rhett & Link: Commercial Kings* premiered in June 2011. By showcasing their unique sense of humour and creating a clear point of view online, Rhett and Link used their videos to find opportunities in new media and television.

Other examples

Actor/director Mark Gantt created the web series *The Bannen Way* for the Sony-owned distribution site Crackle. He has since used the success of that project to work in other prominent web series such as *Leap Year*, *The Guild* and *Suite 7*. Director Scott Brown used his web comedy *Blue Movies* to find representation and work creating web content for the Spike TV series *Blue Mountain State* and supplemental material for the feature film *The To Do List*. Writer Woody Tondorf's series, *Elevator*, and other web videos served as a calling card to find a job on the writing staff for the Hulu series *The Morning After*.

Opportunities in new media for content creators, producers and actors continue to grow. Hulu, Yahoo and Crackle have demonstrated a commitment to developing original, exclusive online series. Some of these programmes hail from well-known names like Ben Stiller, Vin Diesel, and Zooey Deschanel (*Burning Love*, *The Ropes* and *The Single Life*, respectively). Web series can also present an opportunity for artists to take the next big step in their careers, as with JD Walsh, the creator and first-time director of the Hulu original series *Battleground*.

DEVELOP A TELEVISION PROPERTY

Many web series find success because of how *different* they are from traditional TV shows. They can feature choppy editing and over-the-top acting, deal with topical subjects almost instantaneously, and are usually forgiven for mediocre production quality – aspects that usually are not acceptable in traditional media.[12] However, if you specifically hope to have your web series adapted into a television show, then it should look and feel as much like its intended format as possible.

For example, you must show that there is enough depth in your idea to last a hundred or so TV-length episodes. To this degree, it is important to demonstrate what genre your series fits into – whether that be a procedural drama, primetime soap, reality contest or game show. Define the parameters of your concept and make the show that you would like to see on the air, just in an abbreviated format.

Case study

In 2007, *Stargate: SG-1* co-executive producer Damian Kindler created and produced eight episodes of an original web series called *Sanctuary*. The show was shot almost entirely in front of a green screen with CGI-created backgrounds. Its unique look and significant number of online viewers attracted the attention of the Syfy cable network, which repurposed the initial episodes to launch an hour-long television show. Damian was able to bring his entire cast and production team with him, and translated success online into sustainability on TV: *Sanctuary* has been on the air for four seasons now.

Other examples

As you have surely noticed, most TV shows feature actors and actresses with a certain amount of name recognition. Many examples of web series that have made the jump to television also have name talent involved: Lisa Kudrow stars in *Web Therapy*, which has been picked up by Showtime, Rob Corddry is in the series *Childrens Hospital*, which is now on Cartoon Network's Adult Swim, and Kiefer Sutherland headlines the web series *The Confession*, which is being developed into a feature film by Image Entertainment. Attaching a notable star to your web series is not required to make future deals, of course, but it is an element to consider when deciding what goals are reachable for your particular production.

BE INFORMATIVE

The tools of new media can be used not only to entertain, but to share information regarding a cause, underreported news story, local events, or whatever else you feel passionate about. A web series can be used to educate, inspire, and build a grassroots community of support. You should always make sure, to the best of your abilities, that any information you provide in such videos is up-to-date and accurate.[13]

The requirements and resources for sustainability of an informative web series include the same options as previously discussed. Targeting brands and distribution platforms that share your project's mission can lead to partnerships that finance future episodes. If you produce these types of shows in conjunction with a non-profit company (or start your own), you have the additional ability to solicit donations from your viewers to continue production. There are also a number of private and government grants available to creators seeking to provide public educational services.

Case study

The non-profit organisation StoryCorps was founded in 2003 by David Isay with the mission to preserve an oral history of everyday Americans. To date, StoryCorps has recorded over 30,000 interviews with over 60,000 participants that are preserved in the Library of Congress. Like many non-profits, the company receives its funding through generous donations and grants from foundations like the Corporation for Public Broadcasting.

In addition to publishing CDs and books of these recordings, StoryCorps also works with talented artists Mike and Tim Rauch to produce an animated, Emmy-nominated web series depicting select interviews. These stories are touching, funny, endearing, and inspiring. In recognition of the tenth anniversary of 9/11, StoryCorps commissioned a series of videos featuring interviews with those who lost loved ones in the tragedy. It is a profoundly moving series.

Other examples

The PBS series *Off Book* works to inform the public about new art projects and trends, with an aim to create a broader art-appreciating community online. Morgan Spurlock (*Supersize Me*) hosts a show on Hulu called *A Day in the Life* that profiles dynamic individuals from a variety of backgrounds.

Like talk radio, web series can also be used to filter news with political ideologies. Glenn Beck moved his conservative talk show from the Fox News cable network to the web via a viewer subscription service. The liberal/progressive talk show *The Young Turks* has grown its following online and can now additionally be seen on the Al Gore co-founded Current TV network.

So, what will the goal of your web series be? What parameters will you use to define success? As you will see in the next chapter, the development process is informed by the requirements needed to achieve your stated goals. These objectives determine your budget constraints, cast and crew considerations, and time commitment.

Your series can most definitely be successful, but it will require a certain amount of work to get there. Consider the investments that our case study creators put into their shows in order to achieve success. Before you embark on this exciting endeavour, make sure that you are prepared to do the same. This book will provide you with all of the tools and resources you need, but only you can provide the passion, determination and work ethic necessary to achieve success.

INTERVIEW WITH MICHAEL CYRIL CREIGHTON

Michael Cyril Creighton is a New York-based actor and writer. He created, writes and stars in the comedy *Jack In a Box*. The show won Best Web Series at the 2010 New York Television Festival and Michael received a Writers Guild nomination in 2012 for Outstanding Achievement in Writing

Original New Media. Since *Jack In a Box* launched in 2009, Michael's goals for the series have evolved. What began as a one-video project has now become a four-season series.

How did Jack In a Box first come about?

I had done some projects on the web before. I used to do video podcasts on VH1 for *Best Week Ever*. When that ended, I wanted something else that I could work on. The first episode of *Jack In a Box* was just me. It was only going to be a teaser for something I was going to do later. I knew up front what I wanted it to look like. It was really easy to do. Then, when we put it up, the response was great. More than any of the others, the first episode got me an audience.

Because of that response to the first episode, I felt like I had no choice but to keep making them. The first episode was supposed to be a teaser for a project that I was going to write later on – but I was procrastinating. When people caught onto [the first episode], that kicked me into gear.

Did the director of the project have any experience working on a web series?

Marcie Hume – who directed and edited the first episode – had done stuff on the web before, and actually came from a documentary film background. She shot the first two episodes, and the fourth, then moved to London. Then my co-producer, Jim Turner, took over, picked up where she left off, and added his own twist to things.

I don't know anything about cameras. I know how to write, I know how to act, I know how to tell other people how to act. But I didn't know about cameras, and [Marcie] really established the look of the show right away.

How do you keep costs low and find production help to maintain a sustainable series?

I would just use places that were donated. I would reach out to actors and make sure I could work around their schedules. I kept all the shoots really short. I was lucky to have some really great actors in the show, and I don't think I would be able to do that if I had a five-hour shoot. So we try to keep people's time to under an hour or an hour and a half.

Our production [costs] are low, but I think it looks the way I want it to look. And because we're not setting up a lot of lights and shooting from a lot of different angles, we're able to keep people's time on set low.

Do you write new episodes around actors and locations that you are able to work with?

A lot of the time, I do write scenes for specific people. I will check to see if they are interested and available, I'll have an idea in my head, and then I'll write the episode to work around their schedule. I've been really lucky to work with everyone that I've written for.

Do you write all the episodes for a season at once?

No, not at all. I would write as many as I could and then build from there. I also like to know what the audience reaction is to new characters, and then build from there.

Do you have an example of fan comments that have influenced future episodes?

Well, I specifically didn't want to make this a specifically gay web series. I think it was always obvious the character was, but we didn't address it until the twentieth episode. I knew that people wanted him to have some sort of love connection. So that happened organically. I wrote it the way I wanted to write it, though. [My character, Jack] went on this really awkward first date and now he's dating this guy – and a lot of people are responding to that. Some people aren't, though, because they don't like seeing the character happy. Which I get. But, as a writer, this process has been about me challenging myself.

What methods work best for you to engage your viewers?

On Facebook mostly. I appreciate all kinds of feedback, but it's never going to be the same from person to person. I definitely use Facebook, though, as a tool to hear what people are thinking.

Are there other fan reactions that surprised you?

There was a whole season where [Jack] wasn't working in a box office. That was probably one of my favourite seasons. But it was a problem for some people who liked him better in a work situation. But that's not what I was interested in. The first season was work exclusively, the second season was about his personal life, and then the third season fit those two together. I like playing with expectations – what it means to be in a box.

What is the most challenging part of gearing up for production on a new season?

Scheduling. Figuring out time to do all this while working a full-time job and auditioning for other projects. It's sometimes hard to balance things.

Is it easy to keep your cast and crew motivated for production?

Absolutely. We have a great time when we're [in production]. And I couldn't be more thankful for everyone that's been involved with [the project].

Has creating your own web series opened up other opportunities for you in new media?

There is a great community of people here in New York. It's a pretty scrappy group of people who are really motivated, and everyone is pretty game to work with other people. I've worked with Thom Woodley (*The Burg*). I did an episode of *Very Mary-Kate* and an episode of *Downsized*. It's a great way to work because it's usually pretty fast. You just go somewhere for a couple hours and shoot.

If you were to produce a new project, are there any lessons that you would take from Jack In a Box, moving forward?

The thing that I think is most important is keeping the costs low and the time commitments as short as possible. The web isn't TV – and that's what's great about it. Why spend a TV budget – or even a portion of a TV budget – on a web project? I think there are ways to make things look good for very little money, not make yourself go broke, and give yourself a tool that you can use to work on other projects. And always have a good time.

Also, to me, an important thing is casting. Having really good actors. Mostly everyone [appearing in *Jack In a Box*] I know, I have worked with before. I generally surround myself with people that I know, that I'm comfortable with. That puts me more at ease, because I'm always worrying about if I'm acting okay. So I will cast people that I know will get it, and I don't have to hand-hold anybody.

3. DEVELOPING THE IDEA

The goal of any filmmaker should be to tell a great story. This is true no matter the medium, and certainly applies to web series. However, as a web series creator, you are tasked with much more than accomplishing this single objective. It is your job to craft an entire franchise.

It is your job to create dynamic characters, an engaging format, and a compelling narrative that can carry on through dozens of episodes. In addition to these creative considerations, you must also be practical during the development process. Depending on your series' specific goals, marketing potential and sustainability requirements must also be taken into account.

This chapter of the book will guide you through the development process by helping you find potential concepts and articulate your specific vision. Then you will be able to confirm that your idea works appropriately towards the goals for your series as defined in the previous chapter. Also, it will be important to answer the question: 'Why the web?' Why is a web series the best medium for your concept, and how can you creatively use the internet for your franchise? Finally, this chapter will help you to write the script – or outline the non-scripted format – so that you can move onto the next steps in pre-production.

Creating an original web series is an ambitious undertaking. Developing your concept, though, is the least expensive part of the process. By taking the time to focus on this initial phase, you will be able to reduce your risk going forward.

INSPIRATION

The first step in development is to come up with your series concept. It is time to find that spark of an idea. Of course, inspiration can strike at any time and it is important to be creatively open-minded. There are no bad ideas at this stage, so keep a notebook handy and write down whatever comes to mind. Then take these broad concepts to the 'Definition' and 'Reflection' phases that follow to determine whether or not to move forward into further development. To get the creative juices flowing, so to speak, consider some of the questions below.

What interests you? You do not necessarily have to write about what you know. But you should definitely write about something that interests you. Passion for a topic is hard to fake, and it is also hard to hide. If you have a genuine fascination and love for a particular arena, then that enthusiasm will likely spread to your production team and ultimately to your viewers. Inversely, do not develop an idea that you do not particularly care about just because you feel it may have marketing potential. If there is one thing that internet users do well (and seem to take pleasure in), it is sniffing out phonies. The best way to engage an audience is to speak to them as a peer about a common interest.

What unique resources do you have access to? You do not want to think too much about the production logistics of your web series at this stage, but it is worth considering what types of equipment, locations, activities and actors you have easily at your disposal. Specifically, think about available resources that would set your series apart from other online shows. Do you live next to an out-of-the-ordinary location? Are you friends with an improv comedy team? Do you have a vintage car in your garage? Sharing some of the things in your own life that you may take for granted can potentially contribute to a compelling web series.

What are some specific talents that you have? As the producer and possible star of your web series, brainstorming show ideas should also include some self-reflection. Do you know how to make an animated or stop-motion video? Are you crafty with special effects? Can you compose and sing funny songs? One of the best ways to make a show uniquely yours is by letting the series be a reflection of your own individual personality.

Where do you spend your time online? Put yourself in the shoes of your potential internet viewer. What types of websites do you like to visit? The blog topics and humour sensibilities of these sites may be sources of inspiration.[14] Your series does not have to draw so specifically from an existing site, but popular online formats can be great launching points for your own unique premise.

Who do you like hanging out with? Ultimately, people watch shows with characters that they enjoy spending time with, whether it is a person who makes them laugh, lives a life they wish they had, or is simply someone they love to hate. Think about the intriguing, funny and slightly bizarre people in your own life. Then ask yourself: would any of them make compelling characters in a web series?

What worlds do you want to know more about? 'Worlds', in this case, can mean any number of things: an occupation, a location, a time period, an event, or even a fictional universe. Creating a web series is about establishing a particular world, and then returning there episode after episode. The more interesting a place you create, the more opportunities you have to tell compelling stories there. Think about unusual jobs that some people have, a wild time in history, or a crazy place you ended up one weekend and could not wait to tell your friends about. Then, of course, consider: could this be a cool setting for a web series.

What types of shows do you wish were on the air? Again, it never hurts to brainstorm from the perspective of the fan. What kinds of shows would you watch, if they were available? Are there cancelled shows that you wished were still on the air? Do you miss a genre that seems to have disappeared? Creative executives and producers call this process 'identifying holes in the marketplace', but that often comes from a purely business-minded point of view. Instead, try to answer this question from the standpoint of wanting to entertain yourself first. After all, if you wouldn't watch your show, why would you expect anyone else to?

Finally, sift through your bounty of ideas and try to select the two or three that you feel most strongly about. Choose concepts that truly excite you. There will be plenty of time to think like a producer in the later steps. For now, think like a writer, be as creative as possible, and trust your instincts.

DEFINITION

Your ideas at this point surely have varying degrees of detail. The next step in the development process is to format your concept into a succinct pitch. In order for a writer or producer to sell a show, they must deliver what is essentially a sales pitch to the prospective buyer. For the purposes of this section, you need not try to sell the series with your pitch. Instead, focus on conveying precisely what your imagined show will be so that you can accurately evaluate its potential in the 'Reflection' section to follow. Delivering the pitch to a few friends can help you form the clearest articulation of your series, and answering their questions can help you to fill in any holes in your concept.

Deliver the premise

The beginning of your pitch, with only a few sentences, should explain what your series is all about. This very brief summary is your show's logline, and captures the core elements of your concept. You do not have to answer every question below, but as much as possible try to convey:

- What is the genre? Scripted or non-scripted? Comedy or drama?
- Generally, who are the characters and where does the show take place?
- What is the format of each episode? Is there a unique stylistic element?

- Is there a larger arc to the series, or is each episode self-contained?

Example (as an example, excerpts from a single pitch document are included with each part of this section):

SPELUNKING is a send up of the *Quantum Leap* format, with a postmodern twist. Instead of leaping into actual events from the past, our heroes – two 20-something roommates – are transported into different genres of feature films and television shows.

Define the world

After the condensed version of your series, you can provide more details of the show's setting, format, tone and style. As discussed previously, the world of a series can be the location and time period of the narrative. Be as detailed as needed, depending on the complexity of your show's setting. Provide any background information that the audience will need to understand the action moving forward.

Additionally, defining the world includes describing the format of the series. Some shows reach satisfying conclusions at the end of each episode, while others have narratives drawn out over an entire season. Sketch shows and anthologies, for example, usually feature self-contained episodes that are connected only by recurring themes or characters. Reality and competition shows are also defined by their format, so that the audience generally knows what to expect each episode.

Your series' tone comes from your point of view as the storyteller and the feelings that you are trying to convey to your audience. The tone of any show is important and should be as specific as possible. If your goal is to make the audience laugh, then what are your sensibilities? Are you relying on parody, absurdist or gallows humour, for example? By clearly stating your show's tone, you help determine which types of situations and storylines would have a place in your series, and which simply do not belong.

Lastly, you can consider including style notes into your pitch. What aesthetic elements are unique to your series? These can include technical as well as storytelling components. Perhaps your series is shot to resemble a video blog, like the testimonial and confession in the Italian series *L'Altra*, or is composed of amateur 'found footage' videos like *The Apocalypse Diaries*. Or maybe the story takes place in real time, such as *00:24* (a parody of Fox's *24*). These details will help define the look and feel, as well as the structure of each episode and the series as a whole.

Example

One night, roommates Logan and Suzy are home at their apartment together. Logan has ordered this crazy new device from who-knows-where – the *Spelunker 6G* – and is syncing it up with all his other tech gadgets. And, through a method that will be explained via an awesome 80s-style theme song, they are sucked into the digital world.

Logan and Suzy will find themselves in all kinds of movies and shows – gritty crime dramas, romantic comedies, old Westerns, *Twilight Zone* episodes, game shows, you name it. And, like *Quantum Leap*, it's their goal to complete whatever storyline they land in so that they can jump to the next one, hoping each leap will be their last…

Introduce the characters

As simply as possible, convey the physical and personality traits of your major characters, then clearly define the goals of each. Setting these objectives will motivate the narrative, as the audience watches your characters achieve success, fall short, or change their goals altogether. Lastly, consider what kinds of obstacles – whether they be external forces, or having to overcome character flaws – each will encounter throughout the series.

Example

LOGAN WAGNER – He's one of those film-school geeks who loves old movies and watches way too much television. He's also a tech-nerd, so he's got the latest digital gizmos to stream videos anywhere he wants. And he's recently discovered that he may have fallen in love with his roommate.

SUZY OCHOA – An artistic hipster-type who deplores anything mainstream. She likes to think she lives way too out-of-the-box for most pop-entertainment.

Expand the series

With the major components of your series defined, you can now discuss the episodes themselves. Use all of your previous information to explain what will happen in the pilot episode. Then, expand the story to include the entire first season. Provide some specific episode ideas, if possible. By working to the conclusion of your pitch, you should have a very precise idea of your series' scope.

Example

Logan and Suzy will have to catch the bad guys. Make sure a couple falls in love. Rescue the damsel in distress. And they have very different ways of doing that. Logan knows all the genre conventions, so he loves saying things like, 'Oh, this is the part where...' and trying to do things the way he's seen them done a million times before. Suzy, meanwhile, likes to be more unconventional. Why does a Western have to end in a shootout? Will this rom-com couple really be better off together? Maybe the best endings aren't the ones we think of first, she'll say. And sometimes she'll be right.

REFLECTION

Once you have a fully formed concept and have practice-pitched the idea enough to be comfortable with all its elements, the next step will be to cross-reference with your ambitions as defined in the previous chapter. Can your proposed web series best help you to reach your goals?

Have fun

Especially if this is the first project you have ever produced: keep costs low and create a situation where people are enthusiastic to work with you. Your concept should be easy to shoot, relying mostly on equipment, locations and props that you already own or have free access to. The subject matter can, of course, be anything you like, but topics that you already spend time pursuing make the most sense, for this reason. Finally, you can get away with not paying cast and crew if you promise to deliver a unique finished product, value creative collaboration, and are respectful of people's time.

Make this your full-time job

If your intent is to make revenue via pre-roll and pop-up advertisements (whether as a YouTube partner or through another distributor), then you will need to develop a concept that allows you to generate content several times a week. Simple sketch comedy shows like 5 *Second Films* are able to post new shows every weekday. Video blogs or personality-hosted shows comment on the latest trending topics[15], which helps to generate new material and provides promotional support. Again, these shows should be relatively inexpensive to produce, and be able to be produced, edited and posted in a short amount of time.

If this is a project that you would like to find a sponsor for, you should consider if the series is 'brand friendly'. That is, do the concept and themes correspond with the types of messages that companies are trying to convey about their products? Does your show target a specific audience that advertisers would like to reach? And, finally, can you produce your show with a high production value that brands would want to be associated with?

Financial considerations are the most important with this goal. The critical aim for your series in this case is sustainability: growing a web series brand so that it eventually generates enough income that it pays for its own production and you can afford to make producing it your primary job. Calculating budget requirements, fundraising methods, and various revenue streams will be covered in detail later in the book. At that time, you will be able to more accurately assess the financial potential of your series. For now, consider simply: is this an idea that you feel passionately enough about to pursue full-time?

Create a portfolio piece

With no necessity for quantity or frequency of episodes, and no brand agendas to adhere to, you can focus all of your attention on the filmmaking craft itself. Decide first upon which types of work you would like to solicit with your portfolio piece, and then make sure that your concept showcases the talents needed for these jobs. Build the show's story around the technical prowess you want to exhibit. Concentrate on quality and professionalism; do not try to produce a show that will look cheap or poorly produced because of your limited resources.

Develop a television property

The initial episodes of your web series may only be a few minutes long, but the viewer should be able to imagine the format extended into half- or one-hour episodes. What networks is your show appropriate for? Your concept should stay within these networks' brands, but not too-closely resemble a show that is already on the air. Can your concept be easily categorised as a crime drama, medical procedural, family soap, or workplace comedy, for example[16]? The intent is to make the parallels between your web series and a potential *television* series as close as possible for potential buyers.

Be informative

If your goal is to educate an audience about a specific topic, then the concept of your series has mostly been decided upon already. Consider developing the format in conjunction with a news outlet or non-profit organisation that might be interested in helping you spread your message.

UTILISING THE 'WEB' IN 'WEB SERIES'

Once you are confident that your series concept has strong potential to help you reach your intended goals, the final question to ask is: 'Why the web?' More specifically, 'Is a web series the best medium for this concept?' *Lawrence of Arabia* can only be imagined as an epic feature film. There should be good reasons that your tale can best be told online.

Storytelling

Sketch comedy plays very well online. The set-up and punch-line format of these shows works great in an abbreviated format; many sketches would lose their humour if bloated to a full half-hour or more. Plenty of other genres can be successfully executed as traditionally short webisodes, but their storytelling methods should take their brevity into account. Think about how your concept could benefit by an efficient dialogue, faster pace and a truncated narrative.

Generating buzz

The double-edged sword of distributing content online is that, while you have the ability to reach a potentially limitless audience, you must compete with a seemingly limitless amount of distractions. Make sure that your web series can cut through the internet clutter. Think about how your concept and execution can grab an audience's attention. Likewise, what will you do to compel your viewers to share your videos with others? Also consider if your concept is relevant; is this an arena that is currently in the public's interest?

Engaging the audience

More than any other medium, web series allow content creators to receive feedback from, and interact with, their viewers almost instantaneously. This is part of the appeal for an audience, too: having the opportunity to communicate with writers, directors and actors. Think about ways to enhance the viewing process and bring your audience into the world of your show. Successful web series cultivate a community of fans by involving them in the creative process whenever possible.

Transmedia opportunities

One way to engage your audience is by creating and enhancing the *transmedia* experience. Yet another industry buzz word, transmedia refers to carrying your show's world and narrative throughout multiple digital platforms. Beyond the initial episode videos, some series have Facebook profiles and Twitter profiles in which their characters interact with fans. Others create original games or apps to correspond with their shows. With your audience already online, think of ways to continue the show's experience in ways beyond simply watching videos. Try to give your fans the opportunity to be active users instead of merely passive viewers.

WRITING

Web series, as the name implies, are very similar in execution to television series. Some in the industry prefer the term 'Web TV' for this very reason. As discussed, online shows have important distinctions from their TV counterparts, but, when writing your web series, you can begin by thinking about the similarities to television. The same basic rules and principles that have been successful there work in new media as well.

Episode and series structure

Even in a short-form serial, stories should have a beginning, middle and end. Similar to the structure of your pitch, begin by setting up the world, introducing the main characters, and establishing their goals in this episode. The story should then track your characters as they encounter various obstacles. Finally, some sort of resolution should be reached, whether the objective is accomplished or not. By either resetting the world to its status quo or continuing the pursuit of an established goal, you will set up the conditions to launch the following episode.

In order to have enough material for several seasons, web and TV series usually have many characters in their ensemble cast. As such, episodes can be structured with a primary (or 'A') storyline and one or two secondary ('B' and 'C') stories that are told simultaneously and focus on different characters. Episodes can also feature a 'runner', which is a storyline without a necessarily developed conflict-resolution arc, derivative of a running joke, that breaks up some of the primary storytelling.

Television shows usually begin with a 'teaser' that is used to grab the audience's attention and hook them into this week's episode. The story is then told through a series of acts (usually three to six acts, depending on the length of the show and network) broken up by commercial breaks. Web series rarely feature ads mid-episode, so your story will most likely be a single act, with a pre-opening titles teaser perhaps. Also, like in television, the end of your episode should encourage viewers to watch more of your show. That could mean ending with a laugh that leaves the audience wanting more, or a dramatic cliffhanger that compels them to return for answers.

The final element to consider as you begin outlining and writing your web series is length. Because you are not restricted by a cable network time-slot, your episodes can be however long you wish. Generally, comedic webisodes are two to five minutes long, while dramas run about four to seven minutes. Of course, this a constantly evolving medium, so feel free to expand or contract as you like. You are under no obligations to stretch your episode's length in order to fill time, so you have the freedom to tell the best story you can in the perfect amount of time. Remember, web series must compete against a variety of distractions vying for a viewer's attention – many *on the same screen* – so be as succinct and impactful with your storytelling as possible.

Formatting

There are a few software programs available to help you write your web series script in screenplay format – notably Final Draft and Movie Magic Screenwriter – or you can format yourself using a word processor. Every writer has his or her own unique style, but there are common elements to every script so that it can be interpreted by actors, directors, set designers, and anyone else on your production.

As an example of script formatting, excerpts from the script for the first episode of *Asylum* are included below, with footnotes following. You can find other examples of web series screenplays in the Appendix.

EPISODE 1

INT. HALLWAY - NIGHT[A]

A pair of BLACK SHOES walks quickly down a dark hallway.

BLOOD drips beside each step.

CLOSE ON: A telephone receiver. The bloody hand
lifts the phone to the ear of a BEARDED MAN[B]. We
only see his mouth, covered in blood, his teeth
stained deep red. He speaks with a thick Eastern-
European accent.

> BEARDED MAN
> I cannot do this any longer. I
> cannot work like this.
>> (beat)[C]
> It is not safe. None of us are
> safe here anymore.
>> (beat)
> No. I cannot leave. She will
> not let me leave. She will
> not let any of us out of this
> place.
>> (beat)
> I will do what-- Wait. I must go.

The man hangs up the phone. We hear his footsteps
echo as he hurries down the hall.

Blood slowly trickles down the receiver and drips
onto the floor. Drip... drip... drip--

> SMASH TO BLACK.[D]

TITLE CARD: "ASYLUM" "Marvin Ulrich: Part 1"

FADE IN:

INT. OBSERVATION WING - DAY[E]

A semi-circle of counters face outward toward glass-walled rooms that line the outside of the observation wing.

DR. SULI URBAN (30s) walks briskly from the hall, flipping through a patient's chart. She'd be stunning if she ever got a good night's sleep.[F]

Trailing Suli is a male nurse, BARTHOLOMEW JACOBS (40s), who's staving off old age with hair gel and highlights.

                    SULI
          Who's coming here?

                    BARTHOLOMEW
          A deputy director from our very
          own Department of Mental Health.

                    SULI
          No, let's do this over the phone.

                    BARTHOLOMEW
          Apparently he's on his way
          here in person now.

                    SULI
          Since when did they care about
          this hospital?

                    BARTHOLOMEW
          Maybe there's a budget
          increase in our future?

                        SULI
              Don't count on it. They'll
              keep sending the most
              difficult cases in the state
              our way. Which I don't mind,
              because it means they leave us
              alone. Until now, I guess.
                   (frustrated; looks around)
              Where am I going?

                        BARTHOLOMEW
              You need more sleep, honey.
                   (then)
              Room Two Seventy-Four. Marvin
              Ulrich, age thirty-nine,
              transferred in this morning.

Bartholomew nods to one of the rooms.^G

                   *   *   *

EXT. ROOF - NIGHT

TIGHT ON: The end of a cigarette burns.
A familiar Bearded Man takes a drag.

PULL BACK TO REVEAL: Our bearded man is
DR. JOSEPH VASILIEV (60s) and he's joined by
Patrick on the roof of the asylum, a vast expanse
of starry sky in front of them.

                        JOSEPH
              Saint Dympna has been here
              since eighteen thirty-two.

> And yet I doubt that anyone
> knows what really goes on
> within these walls.

PATRICK
Information is hard to come
by, I understand. That's why
I'll need your help--H

JOSEPH
I have done my part. I took
considerable risk just by
contacting you.

PATRICK
What risk? You were attacked
by a patient. The greater risk
would be not cooperating with me.

JOSEPH
(shakes his head)
You do not understand.

PATRICK
No, I guess I don't. And until
I talk to who's in charge--

JOSEPH
You would like to see Dr.
Greenwood?

Patrick nods. Joseph takes a small NOTEPAD from
his coat, scribbles something, tears the page,
and hands it to Patrick.

JOSEPH (CONT'D)[I]
You did not get this from me.

Joseph flicks away his cigarette and leaves. Off
Patrick,[J] studying the piece of paper, we CUT TO:

INT. HALLWAY - NIGHT

CLOSE ON: The paper in Patrick's hand. It reads: "613".

Patrick scans the doors as he walks through the
hospital. Finally, he stops at a pair of doors at
the end of the hall.

Patrick notices someone inside the room and, as
he looks through the window in the door, we go to
his POV--

INT. PATIENT ROOM - TIMOTHY - CONTINUOUS[K]

An expansive, empty space occupied by exposed pipes
and thick pillars. In the middle of the room is a
small desk and chair. Seated there is DR. TIMOTHY
GREENWOOD (30s) - stocky, with a buzz haircut and
a strong jawline - holding a PAINTBRUSH with red
paint. He wears his white lab coat and an empty gaze.

Suli sits in a chair opposite him. She leans in,
speaking softly, more to herself than to Timothy.

SULI
I'm sorry I didn't come by
earlier,honey. It's been a
busy day.

Suli puts her hand on Timothy's. He does not react.

                    SULI (CONT'D)
              I still miss you. But don't
              worry, I promise I can make
              you better.

INT. HALLWAY - CONTINUOUS

Patrick slowly steps away from the window. Off
his shocked, confused expression, we--

                              SMASH TO BLACK.

                  END OF EPISODE 1

A 'INT.' stands for interior, or indoor locations. 'EXT.' is for exterior or
  outdoor locations. Sometimes hybrid locations, such as a car, might
  use 'I/E'. Scene headings should also include the time of day.
B ALL CAPS can be used to draw attention to specific objects,
  indicate camera direction (though used sparingly), and always for
  the introduction of a new character.
C A parenthetical between character dialogue can denote inflection
  or intent. In this case, 'beat' indicates a pause in the actor's
  delivery.
D Transitions are usually right-justified, or can be incorporated into
  action as you will see later in this script.
E New scenes require new scene headings with location. Maintain
  consistency in how you label each scene, as your script will be
  sorted by locations to aid in production.
F The script does not need to include a detailed description of each
  character, just enough to give the reader an idea of who this person
  is without slowing down their reading of the action.

G This entire episode's script can be found in the Appendix, but for now we will skip ahead to the final couple of scenes.

H Dashes can be used to indicate that the following dialogue interrupts the previous character's dialogue.

I If a block of dialogue is broken up by action, then '(CONT'D)' is used to indicate that the same character is speaking. Most screenwriting software will add this automatically; it is not crucial that it appear in every instance of a script.

J This is a shorthand way to indicate to the director and editor that a character's reaction shot should close the scene. Of course, another shot may be chosen in the end, but emotionally the audience is connecting to this character's response.

K When following the action directly into another location, 'CONTINUOUS' can be used where time-of-day normally appears; it is assumed that the lighting will be the same as the previous scene.

Collaborating with a writer

You can still act as creator, lead producer, and overall shepherd of a project without writing the script itself. You may prefer to delegate screenplay responsibilities to someone else. In this case, talk with the writer about the series concept, using the materials you prepared during development. Work with the writer to define the characters and choose a story for the pilot episode.

From there, the writer can either prepare an outline or take a first pass at the script. When giving notes on initial drafts, address the plot and characters in broad strokes. Is the script generally on course, or do you and the writer differ on key points of conceptualisation? Give your writer the opportunity to explain his or her choices. You might disagree with the decision itself, but the difference of opinion may highlight an area of the premise that needs to be reworked.

After a draft or two, your notes can focus on specific pages, lines of dialogue, and scene descriptions. Hopefully the working relationship with your writer is pleasant and constructive, but creative collaborations can certainly be difficult at times. Push through any discomfort to write the best script possible. Changing words on paper are the easiest edits to make. Once the production begins, trying to fix the story becomes much more difficult. So take the time to make the screenplay as stellar as it can be.

INTERVIEW WITH CHRIS STONE

Chris Stone is an accomplished filmmaker from the UK who has directed music videos and documentaries for MTV, ITV and the BBC. For his first foray into the medium, Chris created and directed the 12-episode web series *Blood and Bone China*. When searching for inspiration, Chris looked no further than his hometown of Stoke-on-Trent. The town's unique history and Victorian architecture provided a distinctive backdrop – not to mention tremendous production value – for the show.

How did *Blood and Bone China* all begin?

I talked to Rachel [Shenton], who plays Anna [Fitzgerald in *Blood and Bone China*], about doing a web project that would be a bit more manageable, because we both have such manic schedules. We could do it in smaller chunks. We wanted to do something set in my hometown, Stoke-on-Trent. And so I thought we could merge those two [ideas] together.

I discovered that there were some real vampire cases in Stoke in the 1970s, and I incorporated that into the story. This is a mostly fictional story, but it does have its roots in reality.

How did you take advantage of shooting in your hometown?

I knew what resources I had at hand. Some of the locations are within ten seconds walking distance [of my home]. All I had to do was walk across the street, set up, and there you go. Shooting in these museums, you have ready-made sets. I did a lot of research online, and there weren't that many period web dramas being made. I thought that would be a way to stand out from the crowd. And I noticed that American audiences enjoy that quintessential Englishness, so we made it really really British.

What was the most surprising part of the process for you?

I actually ended up reshooting the first episode. We were getting massive amounts of views on the first episode, but then the carry over figures to the next were not what I was hoping for. So, while we were shooting the last two episodes, we went back and redid the first episode. Added a lot more to the mystery. And I had learned so much in that year.

How did you engage your fans?

Twitter and Facebook. We got some press in the local newspapers. We even got some of the actors through Twitter. And some of the props were donated by people who found us on Facebook.

What was your production and release schedule like?

We had produced four [episodes] when the first posted online. So then we were working frantically. We initially gave ourselves a deadline to post every two weeks. But we soon realised there was no way to make that. So it ended up being that [new episodes would post] when they were ready. I'd rather compromise on the release schedule than quality.

If I had to do this again, I might shoot seven or eight and finish those first before releasing any online. But it's still good to be producing while episodes are online, because people see them and might offer their services. You can tweak the episodes, too, based on feedback.

In terms of story, have you discovered things that work best online?

Episode one needs to be your best episode. You need to throw everything at this. If people don't get past episode one, then there's no point. Make the title sequence fun, fast-paced, an adrenaline hit to get people into the story. Ask a lot of questions and end on a really interesting cliffhanger.

I had all of the episodes written out before we started shooting. But it was changing constantly. I had to adapt to the locations and actors that we had available. Rachel, who plays Anna, stars in *Hollyoaks* (a soap opera) and her availability is just near impossible. There was a day of shooting where she couldn't get to set, but I had 30 or 40 cast members ready, all the locations booked out. So I had to rewrite the scene without her there. In retrospect, it actually added a nice bit of character development.

Where did you go to distribute the videos?

YouTube seemed like the place to go. There are several examples of people breaking through on YouTube. *The Guild* had done massively well there. Though it took forever, getting the [YouTube] Partnership really helped. We have been featured on the front page twice internationally, and just today on the front page just in the UK. That got us 30,000 views today alone. When you have the Partnership, you have the opportunity to be spotlighted or featured. You have the option to customise your icons.

How else did you promote the series?

A lot of horror websites. We shot on a digital SLR, and were featured on a site about digital SLR filmmaking. Facebook has been fantastic. The reviews on Indie Intertube were very helpful. All different groups of people watch the show. Various ages. *Twilight* fans. Older generations who remember the Hammer Horror films. Then you've got the steampunks, goths. Then Rachel [Shenton]'s fans. It's quite a mix.

Has this led to new opportunities for you?

I'm teaching a ten-week course on web series. I have students ranging from 19 [years-old] to 80. We work on story and character development, working with actors, post-production. Ultimately, they make a six-minute episode, that's self-contained but could lead on to more episodes. We have students that are interested in directing, acting, some are interested in set design. Hopefully we can set them up so they can continue making their own series.

And what kinds of advice do you offer these aspiring web series creators?

Just go out and make it. Then listen to audience feedback. Constantly keep reviewing the series. If you are not getting the response you intend, go back and tweak it. Essentially it's all about a good story. You can set it anywhere. Tell a great story, with great actors. Write about what you know. Don't make it more difficult on yourself. Work with what is around you.

4. FINANCING THE PROJECT

The question at the forefront of the mind of almost every aspiring web series creator is, 'How am I going to pay for this?' New media panels and workshops continually address the topic of financing and successful producers are almost always asked how they secured the initial funding for their own projects.

Indicative of the constantly evolving online marketplace, this question has many answers and rarely do any two web series go about meeting their budget goals in the same manner. Evaluate the needs of your own show and then use the suggestions that follow to choose which possible methods might be most appropriate.

SELF-FINANCING

The oldest tool in the independent filmmaker's arsenal is to pay for a project out of your own pocket. Plenty of indie films have been financed by directors or producers who max out credit cards in order to get their vision on-screen. This method, of course, is still available to aspiring web series creators. With some thoughtful planning, however, self-financing your project does not have to damage your credit score or leave you in severe debt.

Finding affordable resources

If you are going to pay for your web series entirely on your own, then it is paramount that you be as frugal as possible. Take advantage of equipment that you already own, borrow what you are missing, and only purchase items that can be used in other ways. For example, as you evaluate whether or not to buy a Canon 5D, consider your ability to rent the camera out later or be hired as a photographer for other productions.

Be creative and opportunistic when searching for locations and designing sets. A business may let you shoot at their offices overnight. A closing play may have props and set pieces to donate. You can build your own green screen to expand the possibilities of your own house or apartment.

Students and other aspiring filmmakers can also be great resources. Directors of photography may be willing to donate their own equipment in exchange for experience and credit on a production. Hiring cast and crew for free comes with its own limitations, so be aware that sometimes even the best-intentioned hires might drop out at the last minute in favour of a paying job. Make sure that you can be flexible and accommodating in your shooting schedule whenever possible.

What you lack in liquid funds, you may be able to make up for by trading time and equipment with other filmmakers. Look for opportunities to barter your editing software in exchange for a camera. Or perhaps you can be the assistant director for someone willing to take the same role on your show. Trades like this can be mutually beneficial and lighten the burden on your MasterCard.

Evaluating your investment

Before you put money into your own web series, evaluate the project like any other investment. How much of a financial burden would this be? What else could you do with the money? Some experienced filmmakers advise that you never spend your own money on a project. But if you are able to objectively evaluate its potential, determine it to be a worthwhile investment, and are comfortable with the risks involved – then go for it.

CROWD-SOURCING

A popular, simple, and no-risk way to raise funding for your web series employs a method perfect for the internet: crowd-sourcing. Websites such as Kickstarter and IndieGoGo let users create profiles for their project and allow anyone to easily donate money to the cause. Once you set your budget goal, you have a certain number of days to spread the word and send people to your fundraising site. On your page, you have the opportunity to create a video pitch and provide a detailed proposal for what your project is and how you intend to spend the money you raise.

You are also encouraged to provide different levels of incentives to your donors. For instance, if someone donates five per cent of the project's budget, you may offer them a signed copy of the show on DVD. Or, if someone donates 20 per cent of the budget, maybe you offer them an on-screen credit. The most effective campaigns, though, are those that engage their donors as much as possible and find creative ways to make them a part of the filmmaking experience.

When signing up for either service, be aware that each charges a percentage fee from the money you raise and may also deduct a fee for processing credit card donations. Also, Kickstarter does not charge any of your donors – or give you any of the money raised – unless the entire fundraising goal has been met in the time allotted. If your campaign is very successful, however, you are able to keep any extra money that surpasses your proposal. IndieGoGo lets you keep any amount of money donated, whether you meet your goal or not. (Be aware that the company's fee does increase if you fall short.)

GRANTS

Depending on your country of origin and the subject matter of your web series, you may be eligible for government and private institution grants to help pay for your project. The application process for these funds can take several months to a year, so plan accordingly, and be ready to prepare a detailed proposal for your project. Initiatives for the arts are constantly changing, so be sure to investigate the exact criteria to determine if your concept meets the requirements for grant funding, such as the examples below.

- The critically acclaimed web series *Ruby Skye, P.I.* was partially financed through a grant from Canada's Independent Production Fund, which encourages the production of independent children's series.

- The UK documentary series *The Specials* (winner of two 2010 Webby Awards) was also partially funded through grant money from the UK Film Council's lottery programme.

- Educational and documentary American projects may be eligible for grants through organisations like the Alfred P Sloan Foundation and the John D and Catherine T MacArthur Foundation.

- France has made €3 million available annually to help finance web series of all genres, specifically those that employ new methods of interactivity, through its Centre National du Cinéma (CNC).

PRIVATE INVESTORS

Another way to raise money for your web series is by engaging independent producers who may be interested in investing in a project like yours. There is no specific way to identify these types of people, but they certainly exist. They are individuals who want to support the arts, break into the entertainment industry themselves, have a particular connection to your subject matter, or believe that your series may be a lucrative investment opportunity for them.

Once you have identified potential private investors, you should put together an investment prospectus for your project – much like an entrepreneur preparing a business plan. Drawing upon elements from your earlier pitch document, as well as plans you will make in the subsequent chapters of this book, your project prospectus should include the following:

- *Project Overview.* A general summary of your web series that sets up the other information to come and gets the reader excited about your project.

- *Story.* Next, give the potential investor an idea of what the storyline for your series will be. Though much shorter than a full pitch, this should also include tone and style details to help the reader imagine what you have planned.

- *Production Team.* Who will the investor be giving his or her money to? Besides listing your qualifications and past credits, be sure to help the reader understand why your team is uniquely qualified to deliver the type of project that you are proposing.

- *Production, Marketing and Distribution.* Provide as much detail as possible regarding how you plan to execute your project. Include information about equipment you plan to use, locations you hope to shoot at, and any cast and crew talent you would like to bring onto the project. Without the funding to begin work, of course, some of the pre-production may not be possible to get underway. Let the reader know, then, exactly what their financial support will allow you to do.

- *Why your project?* Lastly, give the reader a great reason to invest in your particular project. Be the best salesperson you can be. Explain exactly what will set your series apart from others and how this can be a worthwhile investment for all parties involved.

If the individuals who have reviewed your prospectus are interested in financing the project, then the next step will be to come to terms on an investor agreement. Odds are that you will not stumble upon a benevolent multi-billionaire who is happy to write you a blank cheque, no questions asked. Most private investors would like a return on their principal and a share of the profits if your web series becomes wildly successful.

You may then need to have an investor agreement drafted in writing. Before signing any legal contracts, you should have the paperwork reviewed by an attorney, an entertainment lawyer if possible. Most likely your investor or investors will have representation reviewing from their end.

In order to protect your personal financial liability, it may also be advisable to form a production company to handle this project. In the US, for example, a limited liability company (LLC) in many cases is the simplest and most appropriate, though you should again seek advisement from legal counsel if possible. An LLC is fairly easy to form through a service like LegalZoom, but make sure you understand the fees and tax implications of doing this before you move forward. Your investors may also want to become members of this LLC, so be sure you are clear in the production company's operating agreement who controls the web series property and how future profits from this venture will be distributed. If you or your investors are not savvy about partnerships like this, then you may want to consider an alternative method of financing.

TARGETING SERIES SPONSORS

Ambitious projects may require financial backing and access to resources that you may not be able to raise independently. Partnering with a profitable and well-connected sponsor to back your series may be the only way to successfully realise your vision. Besides providing a budget that will allow you to use the equipment you need and properly compensate the crew required, finding the right sponsor might also allow you to attach name talent to your series, increasing its odds of becoming a hit.

Series sponsors can be corporate brands that wish to advertise by creating original online videos. Creators can also work with established digital production companies (or new media divisions of traditional film and TV studios) to produce their web series. Video-hosting sites are also beginning to finance their own exclusive, original shows – increasing their brand value much like cable networks have done in recent years.

Because sponsors like these receive many pitches, it will be your job to make your proposal stand out. If you are able to submit materials to a development executive, you should be as brief and powerful as possible. Have a detailed prospectus handy, as before, but prepare a series *one-sheet* that pitches your series on a single page. Potential sponsors should receive a one-sheet that is specifically customised to address their goals and how your series fits into their strategy.

Brand integration

What began as simple product placement in existing entertainment has evolved into the lucrative business model of brand integration. Web series, especially, have become a way for these companies to do more than showcase their products in use; they are a way to create an online identity. When searching for brand sponsors, look for companies that have commissioned original content before, tech- and social media-savy brands, and promotional campaigns that lean heavily on pop-culture and entertainment trends.

Sometimes small or regional companies can be reached through their internal marketing and public relations departments, but most large brands use advertising agencies to handle sponsorship inquiries. Successfully approaching these agencies can also give you broader access to other clients – perhaps your series might not fit with your suggested brand, but the agency may know of a better fit. There are also third-party companies, such as PlaceVine and BrandCinema, that work with producers to find brand integration partnerships.

When pitching your idea and submitting a one-sheet, make sure to emphasise how your show targets a demographic that would use a company's product or service. Also explain how your story and style fits with their previously commissioned marketing campaigns. How does your show convey the company's core message? If this type of media will be a tonal departure for the brand, then explain why you think it can successfully appeal to a new kind of customer.

Production companies and studios

Without an agent or solid industry connection, it can be nearly impossible to get a pitch into the hands of a studio or television network executive. Those barriers to entry are lowering, though, as traditional media production companies are actively searching for new artistic voices in the digital space. The financial commitments required for producing a web series are comparatively much lower than a TV show, so studios are willing to take risks on new talent.

Pitches to these buyers – new media arms of larger studios such as Warner Premiere Digital or Syfy Digital, or primarily web-based production companies like Vuguru or YouTube partner Machinima – should highlight your past projects and credits. Showcase the professional and innovative style that you can deliver as a web series producer. If you do not have a substantial résumé, producing a proof-of-concept video might be appropriate.[17] Any experience you (or members of your production team) have in social media and online marketing should also be featured.

Distributors

Video-hosting sites such as My Damn Channel and Crackle have also recently commissioned their own original series in addition to their acquisitions. Pitching to these companies requires a blend of the concepts used to approach brands and studios. As the primary production company behind your web series, you will need to demonstrate your abilities as a producer. Additionally, you should address how your show fits into the distributor's current slate of programming. (You would not, of course, want to pitch a period drama to Funny or Die. But if your zombie thriller closely resembles one of FEARnet's existing shows, you should address what makes your series unique.)

COLLABORATING WITH FINANCERS

When working with a series sponsor or independent investor, it is important to consider the autonomy that you relinquish during such a collaboration. Whoever is cutting the cheques will most definitely give their creative and production-related thoughts. It will be critical during all phases of making your web series, then, to meet the demands of your financer while fulfilling your own artistic vision.

As anxious as you will surely be to secure your budget and begin shooting, make sure that you are comfortable with the product you have agreed to create and confident that you can deliver on budget and on schedule. Involve the buyer early and often in the development and pre-production process. These stages are the easiest at which to receive notes and collaborate on changes to the series. If your investors feel that they had ample opportunity to provide their input and are satisfied with the plan, they are more likely to give you more freedom during production.

Be as transparent as possible with how much money you spend, and immediately report if you have any delays or unexpected snags in production. Some obstacles are unavoidable, but by being trustworthy and honest with your financer, you have a better chance of securing the additional time or money you may need to complete production. Always be professional and deliver the best work possible. Meeting and exceeding the expectations of your buyer can often lead to more projects in the future.

INTERVIEW WITH BRACEY SMITH & JOSH BERNHARD

American filmmakers Bracey Smith and Josh Bernhard created the sci-fi series *Pioneer One*, which is distributed via torrent sites such as Vodo.net. Bracey and Josh experimented with, and found success, financing their show entirely by fan donations. The series' sixth episode debuted in December 2011 and won best drama pilot at the New York Television Festival.

What were your objectives when you first created Pioneer One and how did that inform your planning process?

Josh: To be honest, our primary goal was to pull off the pilot and prove that we could do it. We were saying that we could do a TV-length episode on a shoestring, and it had a pretty big scope.

In retrospect that was something of a blessing and a curse. A curse because we ended up having to do the rest of the season piecemeal, which made it take longer and cost more than it would have otherwise.

But it was also a blessing because, frankly, we would have had no idea how to accurately plan for producing an entire season without having done a single episode. Breaking it up into manageable chunks, I think, is the only way we would have even attempted it.

Bracey: Our objectives were always shifting to aim for goals that seemed feasible in the moment. At first [we] were going to raise $6,000 to only shoot a scene and then we thought, why not make the whole pilot for that amount? Success ended up being defined in stages. The first objective was to complete the pilot and find a way to continue the show. The pilot was more successful than we had anticipated. We assumed someone would want to step in and fund the show, but instead the viewers did. It wasn't the amount we had ever expected to move forward with, but we thought, 'Eh, what the hell.' So then it turned into finish the season and find a way to fund the next seasons.

When planning for the less-than-no-budget shoots, we would usually act like we had less budget than we thought we had. So the cheapest way to shoot was to do multiple episodes at once. The ultimate goal is to be able to make a living producing a show that we love to work on. I feel like we've had many successful steps towards that goal and are closer now to it than we ever have been.

What has been the biggest take away or lesson learned from the way you have raised money for, and distributed, your show? What insight could you share with aspiring web series creators?

Bracey: As far as marketing and getting the word out, one of the biggest lessons I've learn from our *P1* experience is try everything you can think of to engage the audience, and then try some more. You never know what the audience is going to respond to. Every 'great' idea we were sure of often fell flat and the random things we would mention on Facebook or Twitter would often get a huge response. So it seems to be more of a numbers game than a great idea game.

The web is the world's greatest test bed for ideas. Instead of spending a lot of time and a lot of money refining an idea that may or may not work, you can just try it out and make adjustments along the way. And, as it grows, your audience will grow with it. So instead of having this refined piece with no audience, you'll have something that grew organically with fans proud to be a part of it.

Josh: Raising money is just as much work as making the show itself. If you want your show to have a life, it's not enough to simply start a Kickstarter campaign and wait for the money to roll in. You need to nurture it and actively campaign for it. (Or have someone who has as much enthusiasm for the project as you do to dedicate to it.)

As far as distribution, while we primarily launched through Vodo and their distribution coalition of BitTorrent networks, we wanted to make the show as visible and easy to watch as possible. So we didn't limit ourselves to one venue; we launched on Vodo, YouTube, Blip, Vimeo, and others. I'd say be exclusive to one only if they're making it worth your while with assistance promoting or funding. Don't worry about 'diluting' your viewing figures. Just about every site provides analytics; just add them all together and promote that as your viewership.

Do you have any specific 'if I knew then what I know now' advice that you'd like to pass along to anyone thinking about making their own original web series?

Josh: My advice is to do the thing you want to do, not a commercial for the thing you want to do or the thing you think people want to see. I think there's an attitude that web content is a 'less-than' form, and people limit their thinking. You know that project that you love, but you're saving for when you make it big? Do that one.

5. CREATING A MARKETING PLAN

Many filmmakers enjoy creating content for the web because there is a potential to engage audiences from all over the world. Viewers can discover your show through a variety of means, and effortlessly share the experience with their friends. In short, anyone can find and fall in love with your project.

The inverse of this is also true. As a marketer, you have the opportunity to seek out people who may be interested in your series and give them the chance to watch. In a medium expanding seemingly faster than can be calculated, the battle for users' attention is ever more competitive. If you want to get your show in front of as large a potential audience as possible, you will need a focused plan of action.

The marketing strategy for your series should be part of pre-production, as much as any preparation for your shoot. In traditional media, the general rule of thumb is that for every dollar spent on production, you should spend a dollar on marketing. You may not be able to spare this ratio, but the more of your budget that you can devote to promotion, the more likely your series will be to find an audience. If monetary contributions are not possible, you should at least plan on putting an equal (if not greater) amount of time commitment into marketing.

Successful advertising of your series may include the creation of additional content such as behind-the-scenes footage, cast interviews or video blogs. You may also want to take photos of your cast for use in posters and graphics. Anticipate these needs whenever you can, so that you can most efficiently use everyone's time during production.

You will be trying to engage viewers using a variety of different platforms, so it is important to keep your message consistent throughout. Whatever methods you use to reach your audience, you will be in charge of maintaining and protecting your show's brand identity. Creating an independent web series gives you the freedom to present your series however you like. Of course, it also puts the responsibility of marketing squarely on your shoulders.

CREATING YOUR BRAND

Corporations pay huge sums to PR companies and advertisers[18] in order to create a favourable (and, hopefully, profitable) portrayal of themselves. Branding is serious business. The objective is to present an image that represents not only a product, but also its history, the people who produce it, and the feelings it should evoke in the consumer. It is about selling an idea as much as a tangible item.

Branding your series

The concept of branding applies to branding a web series. Try to distil your show down so that it can be presented in as definite a way as possible. In a sentence, what is your series about? Can you convey this in fewer words? A single word? Exercises like this will help you to create future marketing materials that all work to project the same message.

When users first visit your website, find a description of your series, or are invited to your Facebook page, for example, what image do you want to present? Think about the tone of your series and consider what the emotional takeaway should be for the audience. Are you trying to frighten? Inform? Do you want to make people laugh? Set the stage for your series by preparing the audience to join in whatever experience you hope to provide.

The production narrative

Your goal for building a brand is to help viewers of your series become supporters of the entire project. Serious fans are interested in more than just the production itself. They want to know about the genesis of the project, who the filmmakers are, and how everything was put together. The more ways that fans can connect with a series, the more invested they become and the more likely they are to continue watching.

As brand manager for your series, it will be your job to create a narrative of the production. This is your opportunity to bring your audience behind the curtain, introduce yourself as a filmmaker, and talk about the intentions for your series. Use this narrative when conducting interviews, responding to the press, and generally presenting yourself and your show to the public. When a blogger, for example, is trying to write an article reviewing the series, help them to tell your story.

How do you create this narrative? Think about how you want to position your show in the marketplace.

- *Innovation*. Are you the first show to use a particular production style or new equipment?[19] Being an early adopter or showing that you are on the cutting edge of an emerging trend can put you in a unique position in the marketplace.

- *Audience*. Perhaps your show specifically targets a niche demographic. You may want to focus your marketing directly on this group and grow your online community from there.[20]

- *Similar content*. As important as it is to be innovative and original, you may find the most audience response by comparing your series to other shows or movies.

- *Talent*. If you have a recognisable star or critically acclaimed director, use these names to promote your series. Some filmmakers and actors have fans of their previous works, so it may be in your interest to lead your marketing strategy by highlighting their involvement in the project.

Target demographic

Demographics can be used to generally describe the audience of your series. Characterisations can broadly be made based upon gender and age, or more specifically by race, geographic location, sexual orientation, level of education, or income. The more precise and detailed you can be about your intended audience, the easier it will be for you to make marketing choices directed toward this group.

Are the characters in your series similar to the real-life viewers you believe will be interested in your show? Maybe you want to connect to an audience with the same interests as you. Or, perhaps, you are trying to provide content for a group that you feel is underrepresented in the marketplace. Try to identify these groups so that you can find the best ways to engage them, and speak as authentically as possible.

Graphics and copy

Bold, easily identifiable graphics will help viewers identify content from your series wherever they find it. Preparing a few graphics before posting anything online will let you maintain consistency and avoid confusion with your audience. These images may have to be adjusted slightly depending on their use, but beginning with three strong images is a great start.

- *Poster.* Think about the posters you see in a movie theatre lobby. Use a graphic or photo from production to set the tone for your series. Unlike traditional movie posters, your image will primarily be seen in a smaller scale on someone's computer. Try to make the image as simple and impactful as possible. Avoid small text, especially the cluster of credits most film posters cram on the bottom. Most posters are sized with a 1:1.48 scale; aim for a 540x800 image.

- *Banner.* Websites that you customise yourself often give you the option to put a large, horizontal image at the top of the page to identify your content. The same ideas about conceptualising your poster apply to the banner. Its dimensions, however, are much wider and quite thin. Many banners are 980 pixels wide, with heights varying from 200 to 400 pixels.

- *Thumbnail.* See if you can fit the title of your series or a single, iconic image onto a square graphic. Try to create an image that is legible and identifiable at 150x150, but also at 50x50 and 33x33 (both standard sizes for Facebook posts).

ONLINE PRESENCE

As you introduce audiences to your web series, think about the entire online experience for the viewers. How will they watch your show? Where will they go to find more information about the series? Can they interact with other fans? Maintaining a consistent online presence will help welcome audiences into the world of your series and begin to build a community of viewers. When preparing to launch, then, there are three primary arenas that you will need to focus on branding.

Series website

The main hub for your series should highlight the videos as well as ways for viewers to become more involved with the project. Most users who visit your website have found your show through other means; they have read a review or perhaps watched an episode embedded on another site. That means visitors are already intrigued and interested in your series. Use your website to engage them further.

The episodes themselves should be prominently displayed on your homepage, and easily accessible from anywhere on the site. Bonus content and additional videos should also be distinct. Let users meet your cast and crew through interviews and brief bios. Tell new users about your series and share the narrative of your production.

Besides providing cool new information regarding your series, also give users the opportunity to join in the conversation. Make sure it is easy for people to leave comments below new posts. Let them sign up for an email newsletter that provides updates regarding the show. Or make them active participants in the series. The Seth Green-produced series *Control TV*, for example, asks users to vote on ideas for future episodes and the actions of its star.

Social media

Only a handful of years ago, having a dynamic and functional website was usually enough to maintain a successful online presence. Today, of course, social media must play a part in the equation. Facebook pages and Twitter accounts are almost mandatory for any web series. Both are great tools to announce new episodes, post updates about your show, and get feedback from fans. They also allow users to easily share content and organically market your project.

In addition, these tools can be used to create a *transmedia* experience for your viewers. Think about creative ways to continue the story of your series through Facebook, for example. You could build profiles for the characters in your show to interact with fans. Ask viewers questions related to your show, and then incorporate the responses into future episodes, if possible.

Encourage viewers to follow you on Facebook and Twitter by offering content exclusively through these sources.[21] You can also reward users for retweeting messages and sharing posts. Incentivise your audience to become active fans who want to spread the word about your web series. Some shows offer bonus content such as gag-reels only after a threshold of Facebook likes has been passed, for example.

Distribution platform

Whichever distribution site you choose as video host (more on that in Chapter 9) should also reflect the consistent brand of your series. Having poster art and banner graphics pre-prepared will be helpful.

You should also write a single-sentence logline to describe your show to potential viewers, plus a paragraph-long description. Also have synopses for each episode ready, as well as full cast and crew credits.

MEDIA COVERAGE

Use your series' target demographic – as identified previously in this chapter – to determine which media sources will be helpful in marketing your series. Cultivating relationships with these publications (online or otherwise) can be mutually beneficial. They can help you to reach a potential audience for your programme. News and media outlets want to educate their readers or viewers about the latest relevant content.

Are you trying to engage fans of a particular genre? If, for example, you have created a show about werewolves, you may want to target horror blogs. Perhaps your series features a subject matter that special interest publications cover. Also consider regional outlets that may want to highlight projects created by local artists.

There are also a number of entertainment blogs and news sites that review web series. Tubefilter and Gigaom, for example, are prominent in the new media community. If you are curious to discover which other sites might be interested in covering your show, check out other web series with a similar feel to yours. See if these shows offer reviews or press coverage, and make note of these sources.

Engaging the media

Once you have identified media outlets that might feature or review your web series, you can reach out to request coverage. Have information about your show ready to provide. Prepare an electronic press kit that contains a summary of your series, information about the filmmakers, distribution dates, pictures and logos, and any other content that will help the news site.

You can also connect with the press beyond simply asking for a review of your series. Offer reporters interview access to your cast and crew. Invite them to the set as a way to build buzz about your project before it debuts. Give certain outlets exclusive content for their sites. Try as much as possible to make each engagement a unique experience.

MARKETING SERVICES

As with any element of production, it can be extremely helpful to employ others to help with publicising your web series. For an independent project, you may want to partner with a producer experienced in social media and online marketing. Some individuals or emerging firms will offer free services in exchange for credit – in the same manner you will likely barter for production crew positions.

If your show is sponsored, you may also have to coordinate with the brand's own public relations company. Branded content is used as another form of advertising, so companies want to expose their product to as much of a targeted demographic as possible. Loop PR firms into the pre-production process as early as you can to ensure that you provide all of the materials required.

Some financing models require that your videos reach a certain number of views, or trigger additional payouts when viewer thresholds are surpassed. When audience totals are critical to your sustainability model, you may want to consider hiring third-party agencies that guarantee view counts. AlphaBird, for example, offers a service that promises an audience for a few cents per view, depending on how targeted a demographic you are after.

PREMIERE PARTY

Debuting your series in a theatre can be a great way to reward your cast and crew for their hard work, and also provides an excuse to invite members of the media to watch your show. Premieres can be expensive – renting the location, catering and/or bar service, hiring photographers, staging a red carpet – so try to budget for this expense ahead of time. Do not feel the need to spend lavishly, though. Low-key, intimate premieres can be just as effective, building buzz about your project with their exclusivity.

FESTIVALS

A great way to increase your exposure, make industry connections, and gain recognition for your work is to participate in film festivals. At this point, many traditional 'film' festivals also include categories for new media projects and web series. Some events even recognise these projects exclusively. Screening at a prominent festival can also serve as a no-cost premiere party for your show.

Which festivals should you enter? Investigate the websites for other web series you enjoy, and see in which festivals they have participated. The website withoutabox.com compiles entry information from festivals all over the world. Look for ones that feature filmmakers from your area, or recognise works in a particular genre. Generally, the longer a festival has been in existence, the more worthwhile an experience it will be.

As a start, there are a handful of festivals and awards that you should investigate first:

New York Television Festival – The NYTVF started in 2005 with a mission to support independent television and develop innovative programming ideas. Since then, it has quickly grown and partnered with major TV networks, studios, and agencies to find emerging talent in the industry. As technology has evolved, so too has the festival, which now incorporates web series projects into its official selections.

BANFF World Media Festival – Over a few days in the Canadian Rockies, this festival works to connect filmmakers with leaders in all aspects of the industry. Their nextMEDIA programme recognises web series and digital pioneers, featuring keynote speeches, award presentations, and workshops from pioneers in the space.

Marseille Web Fest – The inaugural event in October 2011 was one of the first of its kind in Europe. Web series creators from all over the world were flown into Marseille, France and spent several days exhibiting their projects, networking with other filmmakers, and attending conferences about the industry, especially from an international perspective.

Webby Awards – Since 1996, the Webby Awards have been presented by the International Academy of Digital Arts and Sciences. The event showcases a variety of internet projects in four main categories: websites, interactive advertising, online film & video, and mobile & apps.

Telly Awards – These awards began in 1978 to recognise local TV productions and regional commercials. Soon categories expanded to all television shows, movies and ads. Recently the awards have also added categories for outstanding online videos.

IAWTV Awards – The International Academy of Web Television was founded in 2009 with the goal of promoting and recognising achievements in web television. Its members include talented artists and executives from across the industry. In January 2012, the organisation's membership voted for outstanding projects and individuals, who were honoured at an awards ceremony in Las Vegas.

Other credible festivals worth researching are:

- **International Television Festival**
- **LA Web Series Festival**
- **New Media Film Festival**
- **Beverly Hills Film, TV & New Media Festival**
- **NexTV Web Series & Indie Film Competition**

INTERVIEW WITH RYAN VANCE

Ryan Vance is the Vice President of Programming and Production for the San Francisco-based special interest video network Revision3. Before starting in 2009 with the company, Ryan worked as a television executive and producer for nearly a decade. He was an executive producer for the G4 network, and also produced programming for HGTV, DIY, Syfy, and WB. In his current position, Ryan helps to create, produce, brand and market an entire slate of programming across the Revision3 network.

What is Revision3 all about?

We are an online TV network. We super-serve a male demographic. Our core demo is 12–34. We serve early adopters, people that are consuming content online. So we cater all of our shows to serve that audience. The company was founded six and a half years ago by Kevin Rose, Jay Adelson, and David Prager. At the same time, Kevin and David were founding Digg.com. The company founded with the launch of *Diggnation*, which was sort of the first successful video podcast. [*Diggnation*] started when Kevin called Alex [Albrecht] and said iTunes is about to start doing video podcasts, we should do one. That was on a Thursday, and by that Saturday they had the first episode up. That is what started this company and really this space. This was pre-YouTube.

The company started with that show, and then launched other shows. I came to the company about three years ago. Since then, we've been building our slate carefully and slowly, focusing on shows that super-serve the Revision3 fan base.

Initially you began distribution through iTunes. What is your distribution strategy now?

From the beginning, the view was to sell sponsorships into the shows and try to get the shows out to as many people on as many platforms as possible. Our sponsorships are in the radio model, where the hosts will talk about a specific sponsor. Like early television or radio, we don't cut away to commercial, the hosts will actually deliver the sponsor's message. That basically allows our sponsorships to go anywhere the show goes.

Now we have over 40 different distribution channels and platforms, everything from Boxee and Roku, to iTunes and Youtube, Metacafe and

Dailymotion. We are always excited to work with anybody who wants to get our content out there.

We have created technology that allows our creators to upload to one place, and then it is published to all of our different outlets. We have created apps for iPhone and Android. We have our own html player, all developed in-house.

With content available in so many different places, how do you brand the various Revision3 shows?

I am a believer in show brand first, and then network brand. You need to be as non-egotistical as possible in this environment. At the end of the day, viewers are fans of shows. We have a slate with Revision3 branding, but we don't require all of our external partners to do that.

We do cross-promote between our shows. We will have guest hosts or collaborations. One of the ways a new show can build an audience is to collaborate with our successful show creators.

You just announced a partnership with Philip DeFranco, you also work with EpicMealTime – what do you look for in independently produced shows like these?

An audience. An engaged, excited audience. There is a new metric that I've started to look at – it's basically a views to comments ratio. You can gauge how engaged an audience is and how consistent they are. It's a more valuable audience for a sponsor and it's a more valuable audience for us. We are audience first, and I've always felt that way. You have to think about who you are trying to serve. Then figure out how you are going to speak to that audience.

Also, obviously the content has to be good. We need to believe in the creator and the producer. How dedicated are they to engaging their audience? There are a lot of people who can generate views but are not generating a true audience. It is very valuable to have an audience like EpicMealTime's or Phil's.

Once you start working with one of these show creators, what resources can Revision3 offer?

We have a full studio here in San Francisco with edit bays, cameras, all kinds of equipment that we can lend out to our creators. We can send out our production crews to creators to help them build their own studios, develop their editing systems, improve their shooting. We have a programming group that develops ideas for new shows. We have our ad sales team that is the best in the business. It's an in-house ad sales group that integrates sponsors into our shows. When a show becomes part of our network, they get sponsorships that begin to drive revenue that is much higher than whatever they were able to make on their own. We have a marketing and audience development group that can help with things like YouTube monetisation and SEO monetisation.

What kinds of shows are you developing on your own?

We are looking to continue to find categories that our audience is interested in – things like internet, digital lifestyle, technology, gadgets, gear, video games, automotive, sports. We look at the types of things that guys are talking about online and think, how do we create a piece of content that will tap into a fan base or community?

Our audience is the type that is willing to go beyond traditional entertainment. We strive to create content that is authentic to them. We listen to them and make changes based on their feedback.

Your shows are all unscripted and tend to be host-driven. Are you looking to explore other formats as well?

Sure. But it's harder to integrate sponsorships into scripted shows using our model. And once our shows start, they tend to just go – and keep going. We don't want to do seasons. We are totally open to trying new formats out, but we have been focused on non-scripted, hosted shows, which have been successful for us.

What distribution schedules have been most successful for you?

Regular content is absolutely critical online. You have to have new content coming out every week, every day – whatever the format is. You will see that successful online creators have had consistent content coming out on a regular schedule, so that their audience creates a habit. If you don't create a habit, then your audience forgets about you. You are competing against so many other entertainment options that people have.

What new platforms and technology are you looking to develop in the future?

There is always new technology coming down the pipeline. We view every screen – any glowing rectangle that you have – as a place we want to be. I think that apps are going to be a huge focus moving forward, making sure your content is on the Android and iOS marketplace. Over the top boxes, smart TVs, widgets. We are creating widgets and apps for every possible screen. We view that as the future.

Based on your experience, what advice do you have for beginning web series creators?

Collaborations are key while you are getting started. Make sure that your content is credible for your audience, as well as appealing to a sponsor. Engage with your audience through social media, make sure that you are listening to them. Interaction creates investment from the audience's perspective. We use the expression 'create a friend base, not just a fan base'. We want the viewers to connect with our hosts and personalities. That is the key: creating that relationship.

6. PRE-PRODUCTION

Producing a web series requires a blend of both independent film and television techniques. Some shows film their entire season at one time, essentially like a feature film, and then break all the footage up into individual episodes during post-production. Other series shoot one episode at a time – possibly overlapping the post-production of one while beginning to produce another – much like the traditional TV model. Still other web series record, edit and post entire episodes before moving to the next, usually in rapid succession, as would a daily television talk show.

Once you have decided upon your concept, secured the necessary financing, and have completed the development process, you should have a completed script for the episodes you would like to produce. The pre-production process will help you to hire a cast and crew, secure your locations and equipment, and plan for the upcoming shoot. The steps in this section will apply to all web series, though in varying degrees depending on the particular genre of your show.

SCRIPT BREAKDOWN

The first step in pre-production is to break down your script and extract all of the elements you will need to collect before production begins. First, number all of the scenes in each episode's script. New scenes, for the most part, are denoted by new locations or scene headings (also called slug lines). Most screenwriting software can do this for you. The final copy of your script with numbered scenes is referred to as the production draft.

Then go through with multi-coloured highlighters or pens and mark off each **character** when he or she appears in a scene, **locations** (including set design elements indicated in the action), specific **props** and **costumes**, any **special effects** (as well as graphics and titles), and any anticipated **music cues**. After sufficiently marking up your script, create a master list of all the elements in each category. Next to each listing, include every episode and scene number where that particular element appears in the script.

To further assist in pre-production, each category's listings can be expanded:

Characters

Specify whether you consider the part to be a leading, supporting or guest-starring role. Include a brief description of each character, including physical and personality traits. This information will later help you to place casting calls.

Locations

As with the characters, include a description of each setting in order to help you with location scouting. Also indicate whether locations are outdoors or inside, and what time of day. Lastly, to aid in the scheduling process, list an estimate of how many script pages will need to be shot at each location.

Props and costumes

Props include any objects that are used by the characters and critical to telling your story. Make sure to create a comprehensive props list so that you have time to borrow, purchase or construct anything you will need. Also list any clothing items beyond those that you believe your actors will be able to provide.

Special effects

With prosumer tools like After Effects becoming cheaper to buy and easier to master, you may want to include some SFX work in your series. Because of the amount of time that these sequences can require, be sure to list all effects needed so that you can plan accordingly – including testing critical storytelling effects so that you are satisfied with their quality before you begin production.

Music

Finally, list any specific song drops and general music notes. Most composers begin work after final picture lock; however, if you are on a tight schedule, would like a theme song, or need an original song for your characters to sing, you may need to commission a score earlier. Licensing the rights to an existing work can be a lengthy process, and may not be possible at all in some cases, so plan time to explore all of your music options during pre-production as well.

CREATING A SCHEDULE

Identify the items on your script breakdown list that will take the most time to prepare. Be sure to also give yourself enough time to hire a crew, lock in locations (including permit applications, if necessary) and find your cast. Leave a cushion of time for rehearsals, if possible, before you would like to begin production.

As you work with other members of your team, having a pre-production schedule established will give everyone clear deadlines and make sure objectives are being completed on time. A schedule is also a tool that you can share with your financing partners to show where initial resources are being put into the project.

HIRING YOUR CREW

Once you have clearly identified the needs of your production and set a goal to begin shooting on a given date, you can begin to assemble your crew. Depending on the size and scope of your series, you may not require all of these positions to be filled. You may choose to do some – or all – of the jobs yourself. Generally speaking, though, the more dedicated and talented crew members you are able to bring onto a production, the easier it will be to run your set and the more likely you will be to have success.

In order to assemble a competent and passionate crew, try to use first-hand referrals whenever possible. Talk to any other producers or filmmakers you know and ask for recommendations, or contact the creators of other locally produced web series that you admire. You can post openings at industry-specific websites such as Mandy.com or at local film schools.

Of course, the broader your applicant pool, the more diligent you must be in vetting candidates. Try to find crew members with past experience in the specific position you are looking for. Contact the director or producer of past projects he or she has worked on. Be upfront about what kind of production you are putting together, the workload and commitment expected of your crew, and what you are able to offer for compensation.

You may not be able to pay everyone on your crew. For those who are donating their time, be gracious of their generosity by including them in as much of the production as possible, do not waste their time and stay on schedule, and show your appreciation via credits and any other shout-out opportunities you can. (Your series' website will be a great way to highlight special contributions. Acknowledge your crew during a premiere screening. Even a round of applause when someone wraps on set.)

If you are able to pay your crew members a daily rate, be sure to formalise the agreement. If possible, ask a lawyer or industry expert to review any paperwork and tailor for the specifics of your production.

It is a good practice to supply half of the total payment upfront and half upon picture wrap. Paying your crew, even at a reduction of their normal rate, is a way to help ensure that they show up for work as anticipated. It is hard to fault a friend who has to bail on their unpaid position to take a paying gig somewhere else.

Working with the actors' union will be covered specifically later in this section, but if you wish to work with crew belonging to any other professional unions, be sure to contact those organisations immediately. In most cases, your production company will need to file paperwork with the union, which takes a certain amount of time to process. Also, be aware that many unions, depending on the type of project, will require that you exclusively hire union members for all applicable positions. Pay scales, mandatory breaks, and other workplace accommodations will be laid out in detail by union representatives and must be followed to the letter in order to avoid legal trouble.

Who will you need to help with your production? The size of your project – more specifically, the size of your budget – will certainly determine how many positions you are able to accommodate. Review the list below to determine if hiring someone to fill one of these roles would be helpful and appropriate.

Producer

An oft-asked question is: what exactly does a producer *do*? Simply, producers help put all the pieces together. They are responsible for gathering all the resources that the filmmakers will need in order to do their jobs. This is what you are doing. If you'd like some help renting equipment and putting up casting notices and picking up lunches, then you should consider adding a producer or two to your show. Some people are able to give varying amounts of time, so feel free to accommodate them with credits such as 'Associate Producer' or 'Consulting Producer'. Unless you are working with a union, credits are ultimately arbitrary and should be used at your discretion to reward people for their contributions.

Director

The director's task is to execute your vision for the series during production. Because you will most likely be working on a short schedule and tight budget, it is imperative that your director is organised and efficient. An effective director has a grasp of both the technical and performance elements of filmmaking. A great director for your show will also be creative with the resources he or she is given, and able to adapt to changes in production at a moment's notice.

Director of photography

Finding a DP who owns their own camera and accessories can be a real cost-saver for your show. It also helps to ensure that your director of photography is familiar with the equipment and will be able to set up quickly during the shoot. After the director communicates his ideas for a shot and goes to work with the actors, it is the DP's responsibility to light the scene and place the camera. If your production allows, the DP might have a *gaffer*, *best boy*, *key grip* and other *grips* (comprising the Grip and Electric department) working under his or her direction.

Sound designer

Nothing separates professional and amateur projects apart as much as sound quality. Having an experienced sound mixer/boom operator on set, and hiring a sound designer for post, will dramatically increase the production value of your series. For modest productions, all of these roles could be served by the same person, preferably one who owns their own equipment.

Assistant director

Since you may be shooting on an incredibly strict deadline, especially if you are unable to return to a particular location, an assistant director can be instrumental in keeping the production on schedule.

The AD (or line producer) is responsible for making sure the cast and crew arrives on set when needed, coordinates between all the various departments, and keeps the director moving so that all of the required shots can be filmed on time.

Production designer and make-up artist

If you have taken the time to find great locations and hire several talented actors, you should consider taking the time to make sure they all look their best. A talented production designer can make your director's shots more dynamic and transform an ordinary location into a visually interesting canvas. Similarly, having a good hair and make-up artist on hand can help to make your actors more confident and comfortable performing in front of the camera.

Production assistants

Guaranteed, you will be supremely grateful for any and all the PAs that you can add to your shoot. Non-industry friends, undergraduate film students, or anyone curious about filmmaking – they all make great production assistants. PAs can offer their help in whatever department you need and are always handy to use as extras. Be sure to thank these hard-working, likely unpaid, individuals at every opportunity, and check that they are able to learn and observe as much as possible.

FINDING LOCATIONS

There are plenty of reputable third-party websites that can help you to find the perfect location for your shoot. However, these companies sometimes charge large fees and/or refer you to locations that command hefty rates. In order to find the most cost-effective location, you have to scout yourself and talk directly to the property owners. Below are some other tips for location scouting. Keep in mind that you may need to return to this place for future episodes.

- Your friends and family may have a house that can accommodate your production. So many web series are filmed in a small apartment – shooting yours in a more unique home can make it stand out.

- Small business owners can also be generous with their property.

- Build your own set by creatively putting up some drywall in your garage. A great production designer – especially someone with theatre experience – can help to construct original sets.

- Shoot outside to add depth and dimension to your setting.

- Consider shooting at the same location during the day and at night. Also explore the possibility of using the same physical setting to represent two different locations in your script.

- Add extras whenever possible to bring a location to life. Layering background noise during post-production can also make an empty locale feel more vibrant.

Once you have found a great location and negotiated a price that fits your budget, you should immediately check with your local film commission to secure the proper permits. The price of these permits can vary, depending on your jurisdiction. Film commission offices can also help you acquire permits to shoot on publically owned land. To avoid high permit and location fees, try moving outside of major cities like London, New York, and Los Angeles (where filming is commonplace and owners are able to charge high rates).

CASTING

As with hiring your crew, one of the best ways to find your cast is through direct referrals from other producers. If you wish to expand your search, you can contact local theatre companies or actors' workshops with your casting notices. There are also online services such as Cazt.com that allow you to post casting calls and hold free auditions at their offices. By carefully vetting all potential candidates, it is possible to find talented, enthusiastic and professional actors willing to take non-paying (or deferred payment) roles.

One of the best ways to help your series gain exposure and increase its view count is to include recognisable, 'name' stars in the cast. Actors that are active in social media are especially valuable because of their potential to bring a pre-engaged audience to your show. Most actors have their own websites with contact information of their agents or managers. You can also use resources such as IMDB Pro to find actor representation to approach with your offer. Though it may be a long shot, an increasing number of actors are appearing in web series – especially for professionally run productions that shoot quickly and offer new types of roles for the actor.

Working with actors' unions

If you want to use any actors that are active members of a union such as the Screen Actors' Guild (SAG) in the US, then you (or your production company) must register with the union prior to shooting. Becoming an SAG signatory can take several weeks, so manage your time accordingly. You will be asked to file your project under the union's New Media Agreement which means that you must use *only* active SAG actors[22], can only distribute your series via digital/new media platforms[23], and are granted the ability to negotiate your own actor pay-rates with no established minimums[24]. Once you have become a signatory, you can register the actors you would like to use for your production on the SAG website. Other actors' unions have similar agreements in place; simply contact the union representatives for specific information.

Working with minors

To fill the roles of teenage characters in your show, it is usually preferable to cast actors that are at least 18 years old. If you must hire underage actors for your project, however, there are additional guidelines that you must abide by. Every country has their own specific labour laws for employing minors, so be sure to contact your local labour commissioner and carefully understand all requirements. Additionally, if your child actor is a guild member, there may be other guidelines to adhere to.

Minors usually have strict hours in which they are available to work. Most areas require the child to obtain a work permit in conjunction with their school. A registered set teacher of some kind also needs to be hired – to provide instruction for school days missed, as well as to independently make sure all labour laws are observed and the child is not put in any dangerous situations.

EQUIPMENT

Yes, most embedded video players are fairly small and may not show all of the exquisite craftsmanship you put into every shot. Still, you should produce your series for those viewers who prefer to watch full-screen, or even stream on their televisions. Make the picture look the best possible, if for no other reason than that it looks great during your premiere screening for the cast and crew.

That said, if you insist upon using a powerful digital camera – such as the RED One – make sure that you have the hard drives and post-production processing power needed to edit and render. Odds are that, if your scenes are well lit, whatever camera you have access to will work fine for your show. Though it is a significant investment, owning rather than renting your camera is certainly preferable. This will make it much easier to produce future episodes and get any forgotten pick-ups that you might need.

Coordinate with your director, director of photography, and any other members of your G&E department to determine what lighting and camera equipment you may need to rent. Most rental houses require that you carry liability insurance[25], a policy which you will likely also need in order to rent a truck[26]. There are many insurance companies that offer short-term coverage for projects such as film shoots[27]. Whatever company you rent from will simply need to be added as 'additionally insured' under this policy.

It is likely that your crew will ask for more equipment than you might be able to afford, or more than is absolutely necessary for your production. Ask questions about their list. Find out if they can do more with less. Determine what specific production value each asset brings to the project before deciding to rent or not. As much as your team would love to have access to all the equipment they imagine, most talented crew members enjoy being challenged. You will likely be surprised by the innovative solutions that having scarce resources brings about.

PREPARING FOR PRODUCTION

The final phase of pre-production is to finalise your actual production plans. This is the time to put together detailed shooting schedules and walk through precisely how each day will operate. You have assembled a great team to help bring your project to life; now is the time to make sure everyone is working together as you ramp up for the shoot.

Test out your camera, including the work-flow process of uploading the digital video to whatever hard drives you will be using for post-production. Being able to efficiently move through steps like this will help you stay on schedule during a busy shoot.

Give your production design team the opportunity to visit the shooting locations, if possible, so they can gather any additional props or decorations that might be useful to a scene. If your shoot calls for any special costumes or make-up, give these crew members a chance to meet with your actors to take measurements and make necessary preparations.

Encourage your director to rehearse with your actors whenever possible. The more comfortable everyone is with the material and working with one another, the better their performances will be on set.

Make arrangements for craft services. Check with your cast and crew to see if anyone has a food allergy or special request. You should have water, other drinks, and snacks available on set, in addition to a full meal for shoots longer than six hours. Providing a delicious, warm and timely lunch for everyone is a great way to boost morale and show your appreciation for a team most likely working below their deserved pay rate.

Go through the script with the director to decide how long it will take to shoot each scene. Be sure to budget time to set up lights, add set dressings, block the scene with the actors, and rehearse camera moves.

Then create a production schedule that details which scenes are to be shot during which days. Again, work with your director (and assistant director, if you have one) to further break down the schedule by indicating how many hours are allotted for each scene. A shooting day should be no longer than 12 hours, with an hour's meal break halfway through[28]. Give yourself enough time to move to different locations, if needed, as well. Also leave time at the end of the day to strike the set and load up all of your equipment.

Also coordinate with your director and AD to make a specific shot list for each scene. This will be used as a checklist during production to make sure that the director has filmed all of the required coverage, and as a way to keep everyone on schedule during the shoot.

Your assistant director or assigned producer should create call sheets for the cast and crew based upon the production schedule, indicating what times everyone is expected on set, including location and parking details, and listing any necessary props and costumes required. To download a call sheet template, please visit: http://www.kamerabooks.co.uk/downloads/

7. PRODUCTION

After all of your preparations, the big day has finally arrived. It is time to begin shooting your web series! Be warned; this will be a hectic time. Almost everyone involved with your show is coming together to work under a tight schedule. Fortunately, you have completed all the necessary preparations. Now, just remember the goals of production:

- *Finish filming*. Your primary task is to make sure that you get every shot you will need to put together all of your episodes.

- *Be professional*. Do not compromise your integrity or the safety of the cast and crew under any circumstances. If you fall behind schedule, creative solutions can be found, but should not involve moving too quickly or cutting corners that could put people in danger or break any laws.

- *Be able to do this again*. Hopefully you will be able to go into production again soon for additional episodes of your series. Establish a replicable production system and create an environment that encourages your team to return for future shoots. And how do you do that?

- *Have fun*. There is a lot of work to be done and everyone knows that. But try to take the time to make sure production is a rewarding process for all involved.

During production, you will be serving in a role that television series refer to as the **showrunner**. You are in charge of overseeing any on-set rewrites and answering script questions. The director should defer to you for any performance or story clarifications. It is your responsibility to maintain a consistent level of professionalism and production value throughout the shoot. As a web series creator, you are ultimately responsible for running the show.

RUNNING THE SET

Whether your assistant director, line producer, or another producer – someone (other than the director) should be responsible for coordinating on-set operations and keeping the production on schedule. This person (for our purposes, the assistant director) also handles the majority of paperwork: he or she should have an annotated copy of the shooting script with all of the actors and props highlighted, the cast and crew call sheet, a shot list from the director, and contact information for everyone involved. The AD should also have copies of applicable shooting permits, waivers for all on-screen talent, and required sign-in sheets for any union hires.

The director is responsible for what happens in front of the camera; the assistant director is responsible for the action behind the camera.

Arrival and set-up

The assistant director (or AD) should be one of the first crew members on set. He or she is responsible for liaising with the owner of the location to secure access to where you will be shooting. The AD should also make sure there is ample and clearly marked space to park all of the production vehicles. As soon as the crew arrives with the truck, they should be shown where to stage and prep equipment.

Besides the shooting location itself, a 'green room' should be set up as a place to hold cast and crew while they wait for their set call. This area should be secluded from the set so that there is no noise interference during the shoot. It can also serve as your staging for craft services. If needed, the green room or a separate space should be established for hair and make-up.

The AD is responsible for following up with any cast or crew members that are arriving late and alert the necessary departments of any potential delays. This person should continually communicate with the director and other crew to make sure that the first shot can begin as scheduled. If any last-minute resources are needed, it is the assistant director's responsibility to track these down[29]. Lastly, the AD should plan for the day's meal to be picked up or delivered so that it is ready when lunch is called.

Shooting

While setting up a particular shot, the director will work with the heads of the various departments to make sure that the camera and lights are placed appropriately, that the set is dressed as needed, and that the actors are comfortable with their blocking and direction. Once instructions have been given, the AD shuttles between the departments to make sure everyone has what they need to complete their given tasks. If a particular actor is needed or the director would like make-up retouching, for example, then the AD should call these people to set.

When it is time to begin filming, the AD usually calls the momentous 'quiet on set'. This signals the sound designer and camera operator to begin and announce their respective recordings. Usually a scene marker is then held up in frame by someone in the camera department (or sometimes by a PA, depending on the size of your crew). Once everyone is settled, it is time for the director to call 'action'.

If there is outside noise, passing traffic, or any other unwanted element that is interfering with a shot, the AD should take charge to deal with these distractions. When a given shot is finished, the AD takes charge in coordinating the next set-up and possible move to another location. As official time-keeper, the assistant director should also make sure that a one-hour meal break is taken after no more than six hours of production.

Wrapping

As the day is winding down, the crew should begin preparing to wrap the set for the day. Whether you are allowed to leave belongings at a location overnight or not, all equipment should be packed away before you leave the set. This allows you to take an inventory and reduce the risk of anything being accidentally broken while you are away.

Props and set dressing that are no longer in use should also be stored. Food and beverages should be thrown away or properly put away for future use. Any items that were cleared out of a location should be returned to their previous places. Be courteous to the location owners by cleaning up after your production and leaving the space in pristine shape. This will pay dividends if you intend to return for future shoots.

STAYING ON SCHEDULE

You will surely have a lot of shots to get to and have a packed schedule during each shooting day. Staying concentrated and on task will be crucial to making sure you are able to accomplish your ambitious undertaking. Stress punctuality and set a good example by always showing up to a location early so that the day can begin on time.

For each set-up, the director should delegate his vision for the shot to the director of photography (DP) and whatever other lighting and camera department crew members you have available. While they are putting the necessary equipment in place, the director should then go through blocking and rehearsals with the actors. Once the DP is ready, you should be able to begin filming.

Your AD should keep a watchful eye over each set-up and anticipate the needs for a given scene. If an actor or production designer is not on-hand when needed, then the AD should call that person to set. Once filming begins, the AD should look ahead in the shot list and shooting schedule to see if elements for the next set-up can be prepared.

Once production has moved to another part of the location, try to wrap equipment and set dressings from the previous shot. A tremendous amount of time can be saved if items are always put back in the staging area. Also realise that the shoot is not finished when the last shot is completed: time must be allotted for the location to be completely wrapped at the end of the day. Again, anticipation is crucial and getting a head start on the final clean-up can ensure that everyone is able to go home on time.

MAINTAINING PROFESSIONALISM

Even if your production is small, with a cast and crew of friends shooting at someone's apartment, it is important to run a professional shoot. Those who are donating their time usually do so in exchange for the chance to gain production experience. Give your team the opportunity to be taken seriously at their job and practise their craft. The more worthwhile everyone feels their time spent on your show has been, the more likely they will be to do great work and return in the future.

One of the best ways to maintain professionalism is by respecting everyone's schedule. Do not waste time at the beginning of a shoot; if you call a cast or crew member to set, make sure they will be needed at that time. Try your best to wrap on time. If people see that you have been productive during the day, they are more likely to stay late if you need to go longer than anticipated.

While moving as quickly as possible through your shot list, always maintain a safe working environment. Give your crew time to safely set up lights and run extension cords. Make sure your actors are comfortable with their movements around a location. Working beyond an already long 12-hour workday only increases the likelihood of accidents.

Come to set prepared with a knowledge of your equipment and an understanding of what you will be shooting. A certain level of amateurism can be expected on some shoots, but, no matter your skill-set, do your best to take the work seriously and produce a quality product. Anyone who spends all day on set wants to shoot a project that they can be proud of.

CREATING A COLLABORATIVE (AND FUN) ATMOSPHERE

Hopefully you have assembled a talented and passionate team to help produce your web series. Take advantage of their unique skills by delegating as much work as possible. Rely on their expertise and trust that they will deliver on your expectations. As mentioned previously, respect plays a critical role in managing a professional set. Give your production team the autonomy they deserve and resist the urge to micromanage.

Beyond alleviating your personal workload, encouraging teamwork amongst all cast and crew members will foster an enjoyable and creative working atmosphere. Remember, you are producing a show for digital media: a young, largely uncharted new medium. This is the time to take chances and be imaginative. Great ideas can come from any number of sources. By being collaborative, you open the creative doors to new perspectives.

Encourage your director, DP and actors to experiment during rehearsals whenever time allows. Ask for feedback from cast and crew between takes. Think about revising dialogue after listening to scenes. As the series creator, the creative decisions are ultimately yours, but input from others – even if you ultimately disagree with their opinion – can only strengthen your production.

You can make suggestions to your director and other crew members, but try to do so in a way that does not undermine their authority on set. Quietly pull them aside between takes and bounce ideas off one another. Innovative minds function best when respectfully challenged. In order to make sure these creative discussions do not derail your shoot and take you off schedule, though, be sure to clearly establish the chain-of-command so that a decision can ultimately be made in a timely manner.

TROUBLESHOOTING

No matter how well you prepare and how well-run your set, you may still encounter some hiccups during production. When dealing with any apparent problems, be sure to stay positive, be flexible, and improvise. Facing adversity well requires ingenuity, and can lead to creative solutions that sometimes even improve the final product.

Falling behind schedule

Even if you have produced a number of projects before, it is easy to be over-ambitious with your shooting schedule. As the hours tick by and you realise you are still shooting the same page of dialogue, you may need to revise your plans in order to film every scene required for the day. Relay any time-management concerns and proposed schedule changes through your assistant director, who can coordinate with the director and other departments.

In order to make up lost time, adjustments might have to be made to the director's shot list. He or she may feel comfortable with cutting some shots and relying on others for coverage of a scene. A complex camera move could be simplified. Or a current camera position could be zoomed in to frame new shots.

If there is a particular sequence of dialogue or blocking that is giving an actor trouble and delaying shots, then you might consider script revisions. The better performances tend to be those in which your actors are most comfortable. Alternatively, see if the director can film the necessary coverage to piece together a complete scene using different takes[30].

For projects that are falling drastically behind schedule, reducing locations may be appropriate. If a scene that was supposed to take place elsewhere can instead be shot on a set that is already dressed and lit, you will save a great deal of time. Depending on your dependence on natural light (and its fluctuating availability), you may also have to consider changing the time of day for certain scenes.

Again, it is important to coordinate with all departments during such revisions to maintain continuity.

Location issues

All shooting locations come with their own inherent complications. Being prepared for potential issues is key. While scouting a location, make sure that there are enough proper power outlets to run electricity for all of your lighting equipment. Test that you can turn off any unwanted house lights, as well as possible noise interference such as air conditioning units and refrigerators. Check that indoor spaces are sufficiently soundproofed from outside traffic.

Confirm all location reservations well in advance and in writing. The assistant director should also keep a copy of the shooting permit on-hand. Before arriving on set, double-check that you have all the keys needed to access all parts of the set in which you would like to film and stage materials. Have an understanding of parking regulations in the neighbourhood; alert your cast and crew of any spots that may get them towed.

If a problem arises despite your preparations, be sure to have the location manager's phone number readily available. Also have the numbers for local fire and police departments, and know where the nearest emergency room is in case of an accident on set.

Location issues can throw several curveballs at your shoot, but – like dealing with any on-set problems – if you are able to think on your feet, the production can usually still be saved. You may need to scramble the shooting schedule; see if you can shoot other scenes earlier in the day until a resolution for the current crisis can be found.

No-shows

Unfortunately, members of your cast or crew may not always make their appointed call times. Sometimes this is just a matter of over-sleeping or a bad traffic day, which a diligent AD can hopefully stay on top of and adjust expectations accordingly. Likewise, checking in with your team in the days leading up to production can give you a head start on finding replacements. It happens – people get sick, have family emergencies, or, especially if you are not paying them, take other jobs.

Whatever the reason, and whenever you get the notice, you should think of ways to find replacement players for your production if needed. Hold onto the résumés and contact information for applicants that were almost hired for your project. You may feel awkward calling someone who knows that they were clearly not your first choice, but ambitious people usually put their egos aside to take advantage of newly presented opportunities.

You can also lean on other members of a department to replace missing personnel. Find out if your director of photography knows any other gaffers, for example, who might be available to fill in. Ask your actors if they know of anyone who might be able to take over a role.

Despite your best efforts, though, you may have to press forward with production without a suitable replacement. Be honest and transparent whenever problems arise, and take these moments to express gratitude towards all of your cast and crew for their professionalism, passion, and – of course – their punctuality.

ADDITIONAL CONTENT

One of the things that viewers love most about web series is their ability to interact with the filmmakers and participate in the show. Fans love to have access to how the series was made, who the personalities are both in front of and behind the camera, and updates about what is in store next. The marketing strategy you planned out with Chapter 4 of this book should address many of these ideas.

This is what makes creating a web series both exciting and challenging: in addition to filming the actual episodes of your show, you should simultaneously produce a number of 'bonus material' videos. You may need to set aside time during the shooting day to record some of these. Also, you can designate a separate person or team to produce these in conjunction with the main production.

Expanding the story

You may choose to produce additional videos that provide character back stories, fill in the gaps between episodes, or continue the narrative until your series' next season. These videos should be shot with a look and a level of production values that are consistent with your regular episodes[31]. Remember, everything that you publish reflects on your show as a whole. This is a great opportunity for an aspiring director – preferably one that owns a camera and is also willing to edit these videos – to gain experience and add to his or her demo reel, and is a relatively low-risk hire for you.

In order to maintain this consistency and quality, shooting narrative bonus material in coordination with your primary production is key. While series filming moves to a new location, you could shoot an additional video on that set – utilising already placed lights, if possible – before that area is wrapped. Doing this requires a second unit crew and equipment, as well as great communication between the teams. If additional people are not available for a simultaneous shoot, you can work these additional set-ups into the rest of your production schedule.

When telling stories that expand the featured narrative, consistency of characters is also important. Actors should stay in appropriate costume and make-up for these shoots, and play the same roles that they have in the series itself. Bonus videos like these are a great way to show a character from a new perspective, but the core of their personality should remain the same. These are also great avenues for actors to experiment and have fun with their performances, using improvisational techniques.

Behind the scenes

Pictures and footage from the set are always welcome additions to a web series. Viewers enjoy the opportunity to connect with the filmmakers and get a peek into the production. Behind the scenes vignettes are also fun rewards for the cast and crew, as a way to remember the shoot and share with their friends.

In order to gather as many useable photos and videos as possible, a specific crew member should be given this responsibility[32]. Later, you can splice together these random, candid moments from production, set the whole thing to music, and share online. Think about other, more focused ways to produce BTS material. For example, you could focus on gathering shots of the cast getting their hair and make-up done. Or feature the crew grabbing their favourite snacks between takes. Maybe you could set up a time-lapse camera to showcase a particularly complex lighting and camera set-up.

Whomever is given the responsibility to shoot BTS footage should be introduced to everyone on set and given the autonomy to independently move around the location while filming. Make sure that this person knows the key cast and crew members, and is respectful about not delaying the primary production at all.

Your behind-the-scenes producer might also pull cast and crew aside and conduct interviews regarding the production. Allow them to have fun with the questions and try to draw out the dynamic personalities of your team members. Of course, make sure that this person has the camera and sound equipment needed to record high-quality material.

Other featurettes

Ultimately, your additional video featurettes should engage online viewers in whatever creative ways possible. Involve your fans in the creative process by directly addressing them during cast and crew interviews. Entice them to stick with your series by giving hints about upcoming episodes. Directly encourage them to send their feedback and share your show with their friends.

Use these opportunities to showcase the advantages of distributing on the web – interactivity with, and accessibility to, the filmmakers are aspects made easier through a web series as opposed to a television show. Try to make the viewer an active rather than a passive participant in your project. Respond to emails, comments, tweets, or even viewer videos that you may have elicited before production began. Although your shoot will be a busy and sometimes stressful process, it is certainly worth attempting to convert viewers to fans.

INTERVIEW WITH ALEXIS NIKI

Alexis Niki is an American writer (*101 Screenwriting Tips*) and producer based in Paris, France. She created and produced the web series *My Bitchy Witchy Paris Vacation*, which filmed all over the city.

You filmed *My Bitchy Witchy Paris Vacation* on location in France. What were some of the challenges to shooting in a big city like Paris?

France has a large film industry and shooting here is similar to shooting in LA or New York. Permits are expensive, people are used to film crews, the city is busy, space is tight, and we have to deal with weather. One thing that might be less of an issue in the US is that we had to work around work schedules, weekend schedules, and vacation time. The city empties in the month of August, and that includes film crews!

Paris plays a central role in the story, which is about a menopausal mom, pregnant daughter, and adolescent daughter on vacation in Paris. We knew we had to get as many exteriors into our story as possible, but we couldn't afford permit fees. One of the work-arounds we found was to shoot some footage with a Flip camera. It made it easier for us to walk around town and grab shots. Some is simply Parisian scenery, but other footage is of the three main actors wandering through town. We wrote a video camera into the story, so the footage plays as if they were shooting their vacation videos.

Luckily, in France an indie production is seen as something to support. The city makes certain concessions to filmmakers, which is how we were able to get our opening shot of our lead actress at the Place de Trocadero with the Eiffel Tower in the background. On the day we were there, a pair of policemen approached us but only to find out if we had filmed them. Apparently, filming the police is a bigger no-no than filming at Trocadero!

Our personal connections helped us secure several key locations, such as a Parisian café, a river boat docked on the Seine, a church that doubled for Notre Dame, and the American Library in Paris. The river boat was a replacement for what had originally been written as a picnic scene. It gave us some protection from the elements (we ended up shooting that episode in December) yet allowed us to see Paris, too. Filming on the Seine complicated matters for our sound engineer. Whenever a Bateau Mouche sightseeing boat floated past – motor droning, tour guide's voice blaring over the loudspeakers – production came to a standstill.

Being an American living in Europe, what do you think are the differences between producing projects in each continent?

I suspect one big difference is in the approach to the work. Here [in France], we really worked around people's schedules, and that was one reason it took so long to complete. In the States, my feeling is that there's more competition for every position, even on a non-paying project, and therefore there's more of a chance of getting work done quickly. But I decided to go with the French rhythm, and, in fact, because we had more time, I think the project benefitted. There are also many differences on a storytelling and aesthetic level that affect everything from pacing to dialogue to camera angles. I think *My Bitchy Witchy Paris Vacation* offers a nice blend of the two sensibilities.

Did you learn any lessons from your project that you would like to share with anyone thinking about making their own original web series?

It will take more time than you think. Maybe even A LOT more time. Clarify your goals and create a strategy to help you reach them. I decided early on to concentrate on making the best show I could and to building an audience. I wasn't going to worry about monetising it. Don't let anyone tell you that your goals are wrong.

Promote from the moment you decide you're going to make a web series. Get lots of extra footage to keep your audience interested between episodes. Either finish editing all your episodes or make sure your work flow is solid before you start releasing episodes. DON'T allow a breakdown in your release schedule if you can help it. Use the interactive quality of the internet to keep your audience engaged. Because my crew was international – my composer was in

Los Angeles and my editor was in Australia – we did a live streaming event for the launch of our first episode. I was blown away by the response. We had participants in Europe, Australia and the US, and we had a great time.

Get to know other show creators and reach out to them for advice. The web series community can be incredibly supportive. If you're having an issue, I guarantee someone before you has had it too! Be prepared to do 100 per cent of the promotional work. If your cast and crew pitches in, consider yourself extremely lucky! But it's not their job – it's yours.

Finally, just do it. Put yourself out there, make a show you care about, and learn how to build an audience. It will change the way you think about yourself and your work.

8. POST-PRODUCTION

After wrapping what may or may not have been a hectic shoot, it is time to see what you have shot exactly. The raw footage will be transformed into your finished episodes through editing, mixing sound, adding titles and graphics, and including music. Post-production may also be a phase in which you must correct problems that arose on set. But hopefully you can focus on enhancing the overall project, rather than patching holes.

EDITING

The editing process is as much a part of storytelling as writing is. Characteristics such as pacing, tone and motivation all once again come into play when constructing your narrative. Using fragments of the raw footage you have recorded, your task now is to assemble a coherent and compelling story. You should bring as much energy and creativity to this part of the process as you did with development and production.

For web series, length of episodes and density of story are important factors to consider. Brief episodes are the easiest for viewers to watch and share; if yours are going to be longer than five minutes or so, then they must be thoroughly engaging to justify their length[33]. During the editing process, experiment with ways to shorten your videos. Think about trimming dialogue, tightening transitions, or eliminating scenes altogether. Consider splitting an episode in half. Even if you revert to your original, longer episode, such exercises will help you decide which parts of your show are truly necessary.

Hardware and software

First things first: backup all of your video files. The raw files should be stored on a hard drive separate from the one you will be using to edit. This, of course, will save you from complete disaster if there is a system crash while cutting your episodes. It can also be helpful to your editor. For extremely high-res footage (like that shot with the RED One camera), editors usually cut using lower-res files and then will go back to the original files for the final output.

There are several software options available to consumers: Adobe Premiere, Final Cut Pro, Avid, or even iMovie, for example. These programs differ in cost and included features, of course. When choosing which to use while editing your show, comfort and experience are key.

The post-production process for web series should be as streamlined as possible in order to publish episodes on a regular schedule. Whatever software you or your editor are most confident using will be best. You want to avoid technical delays (and added frustrations) as much as possible. If this is your first time editing, you will find an amateur program like iMovie intuitive and relatively easy to learn, and it will meet most of your editing needs.

Editing yourself

Once your files have been backed up, download them to the computer you will be using to edit. The first step is to mark and divide the videos by take, shot and scene number. Then watch all of the clips. Mark which takes are unusable because of a gaffe or flubbed line. Flag the ones you like the best. Use the shooting script and director's shot list to broadly assemble each scene.

Whittle away and tighten the edit so it is as succinct and seamless as possible. Then work with the director to further revise the cut. Your director knows why each scene was shot in a particular way, and can clarify how he or she imagined a sequence would be assembled. From these early rough cuts, you can determine whether or not additional footage (pick-ups) will be required.

Hiring and collaborating with an editor

The size of your project may dictate whether you will be editing yourself. Your director may be able to also serve as editor. If possible, however, you should strongly consider bringing a dedicated editor on board. As with anyone you add to your team, fresh creative voices can offer new perspectives and often enhance the overall project. Also, a talented and experienced editor can navigate the technical aspects of editing so that you can focus on the storytelling.

If possible, find an editor with whom either you or your director already have a working relationship. Editing sessions can often turn into all-night affairs. To keep these from then turning into stress-induced arguments, having an established rapport can be helpful. Also consider an editor's ability to construct serialised stories. Your production crew members need not necessarily have worked in the web series medium before, but your editor should preferably possess episodic sensibilities.

A web series needs to have uniformity throughout in how its episodes are structured. Your editor should maintain pacing by transitioning between scenes in a consistent way. Also, the general length of shots and progression from wide to close-up shots should be the same. Most of this consistency tends to happen anyway if the same editor cuts every episode of your series. If not, however, the other editors should use your series' first episode as a template for the others. It will be up to you to manage the consistency between editors.

After an exchange of notes and further cuts between editor and director, you (as the showrunner) should be brought into the fold to offer input and help complete the editing process. Private YouTube accounts or data sharing systems (like Dropbox) are great for sharing new edits amongst producers for additional input.

SPECIAL EFFECTS AND GRAPHICS

Incorporating fun visual effects into your series can be a way to separate it from other shows. Make sure that the special effects are at the same level of quality as the rest of your production, otherwise they will detract from, rather than enhance, the storytelling. Adobe After Effects software and expansion packs are used by many online video creators. As with editing, though, comfort and experience should dictate use of one program over another.

You do not have to rely on After Effects stock footage for your videos. There are inexpensive kits or do-it-yourself instructions available online for setting up green screens. Safely test-shoot whatever smoke or splatter your show requires and try layering that into your footage. Using original effects and graphics will further distinguish your project amongst the competition. If you have not created a particular effect before, be sure to give yourself enough time during post-production to experiment and refine the process.

And if utilising any of these software programs seems like too daunting a challenge for your production, remember that there are plenty of low-tech ways to achieve special effects shots. Brainstorm creative alternatives that you can shoot yourself, instead of digitally rendering. Consider cutting to a character's reaction shot while the effect happens off-screen. (Good sound and an audience's imagination can be very adequate substitutes.) Think about using models, puppets, or costumes. Sometimes homemade effects can add to the charm and enhance the tone of your project in ways that computer-generated effects cannot.

Opening titles

Some web series try to closely mimic traditional television shows in as many ways as possible, including their title design. Show openings can be a way to express the tone of your series through graphics, colour and music. In a medium where your time with the audience is brief, use this opportunity wisely. Opening titles should be nowhere near as long as their TV counterparts – perhaps a handful of seconds at most.

Remember, too, that viewers will most likely be watching on a small window, so make the text crisp, legible, and hold long enough to read twice. The colour of text should contrast with the video, and a solid rather than cluttered background is best. Use outlines or drop shadows to make titles pop even more.

Closing credits

Credits at the end of your episodes are a nice way to recognise all of the hard work contributed to your production. You may be compensating many people via credit recognition, so be sure to deliver. If you take the time to type these out, then also take the time to proofread for omissions or mistakes. Closing credits can also include special thanks to locations and organisations that donated to your series.

You may want to forego closing credits and instead end your videos with information about your website, social media handles, or call-outs to additional content. In this case, cast and crew acknowledgements can be put in the video's description when you post online or in a separate section of your website.

SOUND DESIGN

As noted while preparing for production: nothing separates amateur from professional projects like sound quality. Likewise, rough moments of your series might be able to be salvaged with strong audio work. Plot elements can also be clarified by perhaps having an actor record a new line of dialogue or voiceover. Use sound as much as visuals to tell your story.

A soundtrack can be used to bring consistency to episodes and create a uniform narrative. Music can be used to carry viewers from one scene to the next. Adding sound effects – whether from a software package or recorded yourself – can enhance the power of on-screen visuals. Layering a track of ambient noise from the location beneath a scene can smooth cuts between different shots and dialogue tracks.

You may have worked with a sound designer on set who mixed and recorded audio as separate digital files. In this case, you will need to sync your video and sound files before you begin editing. An even better alternative is to hire your on-set sound designer to provide your final post-production mix. In this case, your sound designer will take your *picture lock* edit and use the original sound files to create a finalised audio mix. Any music or voiceover you will be using should be incorporated at this time as well.

SCORING

As you have discovered with every step in producing your project, creating an effective web series is all about packing the most content into the shortest amount of running time. Another tool to add to your storytelling arsenal is music. A score can quickly establish the tone and mood of your show, and specifically drive home the emotional impact of individual scenes. Music can help the audience understand what a character is feeling, enhance a punch-line, build suspense, or carry the narrative through transitions and montages.

Also, adding music to your project can immediately increase its production value. A distinctive soundtrack can brand your series and make any of its episodes easily recognisable. Just as the visual appearance of your show should maintain consistency for all episodes, music can be used to maintain continuity throughout.

Commissioning an original score is usually preferable to using existing songs. Making distribution deals and selling your web series in various mediums is much easier if you completely control the rights to all of the music used. Licensing agreements can be made, of course, but you should pay particularly close attention to which formats the songs are cleared for use in. Do not use copyrighted songs without permission, especially if you are earning revenue with your show. YouTube and other hosting sites use sophisticated software to identify music, and they will disable your video's audio and report any misuse.

Original compositions

Unless your characters sing or directly refer to a song during the action, music can be added during the final stages of post-production. A composer usually works off the picture-locked version of your edit and adds a soundtrack before the final sound mix. Search for a composer, if possible, that owns or has access to the software needed to record and properly combine various instrument tracks.

When hiring a composer and commissioning an original score, you should both come to terms on, and execute, a music synchronisation licence agreement. This document will give you (as the producer, or through your production company) the right to distribute and publish your composer's work in synchronisation with video of your project. Basically, this lets you use the soundtrack for your film, but reserves ownership of the individual tracks for use by the composer. If you would like, for example, to sell some of these songs on iTunes, then you will need to specify these terms in your licence agreement.

Many composers have wonderful tools that allow them to electronically mimic an array of instruments. Whenever feasible, though, live instrument recordings will tremendously enhance the quality of your score. University students are great resources for finding talented musicians willing to spend an evening playing for your composer. If needed, inexpensive studio space can also often be found through music schools[34].

While working with a composer, it is the tendency of many directors or producers to lay in a track of copyrighted music, and then use that temp score to demonstrate the desired soundtrack. This may seem like a justifiable method of communicating the expected work you are commissioning, but it can turn out to be a great hindrance to the creative process. Often creators will get locked into their temp tracks and can then be less receptive to alternative music proposals.

A better way to collaborate with a composer is to talk through the themes and emotions that you would like to convey through the use of music. Watch the show with your composer and identify the moments when you think a score is appropriate. (Sometimes the lack of music can be just as powerful as a strong cue.) You can refer to other films or artists whose style you enjoy, as a guide for the genre of music you wish to include. Like any of the other talented artists you have worked with on your project, trust your composer to use his or her best judgement without putting unnecessary restrictions on their creativity.

Licensing other music

For various reasons, you may want to use a song in your series that has been published for another purpose. Indie bands looking for increased exposure can be potential contributors, and becoming associated with a rising star might lead to even more exposure for your own show. In this case, you will need to contact the rights holder of this piece and negotiate a licence agreement for use in your project. The terms of this contract should specify in which videos you would like to use the song, for what length of time the agreement lasts, and through which formats your show can be distributed.

Licensing music for film, television or commercial use can be quite expensive. For exhibition on the web, however, you may be able to negotiate a substantially lower rate. As with talent union agreements, you must be aware of the financial obligations that will come into effect if you choose to distribute your show on TV or sell DVD copies.

Some artists offer their songs online through *creative commons* licence agreements. Their websites will articulate particular terms, but you may be able to use their material at no cost. In these instances, creative commons terms usually specify how the artist must be credited and whether or not you are allowed to re-mix or create a derivative score using an artist's work. The terms may also restrict inclusion to only non-commercial use – so, only if you are posting your videos for fun, without ads or ambitions of selling to distributors.

There are several websites that collect original songs and have pre-negotiated terms for their use in online videos. Friendly Music (from Rumblefish Inc) and Audio Network are examples of these music libraries. Some video-hosting sites such as Vimeo also offer music options to premium members. Again, be sure that you understand the conditions in which you can use these songs before paying for a licence.

Lastly, you may be interested in pursuing songs that are in the public domain. After a given amount of time and under certain conditions (depending upon which country you reside in), song copyrights can expire and can then be used by anyone, without licensing obligations. Usually this applies only to the sheet music, not a particular performance, so you will need to create an original recording of the song for use in your show.

OUTPUT FOR THE WEB

Whether you feature closing credits or not, you should consider ending your video with your website URL and social media handles. You may also want to add a post-roll to the episode, similar to some television shows, that previews the action in an upcoming episode. Your episodes could also end with you, an actor, or another member of your team looking at the camera and directly addressing the viewer. These moments can be used to answer questions posted to previous videos, or to give updates about the production and when new episodes can be expected.

Using their annotation feature, YouTube allows you to overlay links onto your videos. Some successful YouTube partners output their episodes with picture-in-picture effects at the end, using these mini-previews of other videos as links. While addressing the camera, other creators point to various parts of the screen where annotations can be later placed. Lastly, on-screen graphics can be overlaid with links.

Export your video to the highest quality that you would like it to be played. Most hosting sites will then convert the video to lower levels of resolution. For example, YouTube features five tiers of resolution:

- 1920 x 1080 (1080p)
- 1280 x 720 (720p)

- 854 x 480 (480p)
- 640 x 360 (360p)
- 426 x 240 (240p)

Uploading at the sharpest high-definition will give viewers the option to watch at lower resolutions after automatic conversion. Double-check the recommendations for the various hosting sites you would like to use before doing your final export. Most prefer a H.264/MPEG-4 file conversion. Also note that projects not exported with the 16:9 (letterbox) aspect ratio – that is, with the standard 4:3 ratio – will usually appear in the player with black bars beside the picture.

9. DISTRIBUTION

During the early days of film, large studios created nearly all of the content. But there always seemed to be a group of cineastes who experimented with the artform on their own. The number of independent filmmakers grew as cameras became less expensive, and they exhibited their work at festivals and small theatres all over the country. Along the way, they influenced the studio productions with their techniques and storytelling devices, especially during the late 60s and early 70s. Today, indie filmmakers are semi-mainstream, as evidenced by the commercial juggernaut that is the Sundance Film Festival.

When television debuted in the mid-century, it did not enjoy the same type of renaissance. There simply was no infrastructure in place for independent creators to exhibit television shows in a meaningful manner. Cable access channels were really their only avenue, and most of those productions looked like they were shot in someone's basement – as demonstrated by Wayne and Garth in the classic *Saturday Night Live* sketches of 'Wayne's World'.

The internet, of course, has changed all that. Now, independent television has an affordable (that is, for the most part, free) avenue to reach audiences across the world. Online, mainstream productions play alongside independent works. The only difference between them is quality. And that gap is closing.

With the distribution capabilities now under your control, you are responsible for delivering your web series to an audience that is willing and interested to watch. That means finding a video-hosting site that appeals to a demographic similar to that of your show. Or you can utilise a service with a large number of users, and engage your target audience within that population.

You will, of course, want to find technology with smooth video playback, that is easy to embed and share. Marketing potential and revenue opportunities will also come into consideration. But, whatever hosting site or sites you select, make sure that you are able to control your show's brand. As the creator, you are responsible for all aspects of your web series. You have imagined and produced an original programme; do not leave the final delivery entirely under someone else's control.

The objective of distribution is to help grow the series, finding a way to attract and sustain an audience that is eager for more episodes. This can be done in any number of ways, but your focus should be on finding the most authentic method for your show. Make sure that you are able to engage your viewers. The web is not a place for static videos. Take advantage of the unique opportunities that online distribution offers.

FINDING A DISTRIBUTION PARTNER

As eager as you are to share your series with the world, the most appropriate first step towards distribution may be to hold onto your episodes rather than immediately upload them to the web. Some hosting sites and online networks prefer to exclusively acquire series that have not been exhibited anywhere else. In order to maximise the financing potential of your series, you should first consider approaching these sites.

Any hosting or aggregation site that showcases 'original' or 'exclusive' videos can be targeted. The popular comedy site Funny or Die is an example, as is CollegeHumor. Many of these companies also produce their own material in-house, but they are sometimes responsive to outside acquisitions. Of course, you will be far more likely to make a deal if your episodes cannot be seen anywhere else yet.

While looking for financing, you may have previously pitched your series concept to an online studio or network. Do not be discouraged if your pitch was initially rejected and you had to find other ways to fund your project. These same companies may be responsive now that you have a finished product to showcase for them. Often it is easier for executives to take a chance with a show that is fully realised, than developing with a young filmmaker.[35]

Having a distribution partner with a vested interest in your project will help tremendously in marketing. These sites usually have large built-in audiences that can be exposed to your show and impact its view-count right away.

Distribution deals

Distribution deals (like many new media agreements) come in a variety of templates. As always, seek legal advice before entering into any binding contracts, and have representation help negotiate, if possible. Specifically, pay attention to the following terms and conditions:

Exclusivity

Will you be allowed to upload your videos to other sites, or does this company have exclusive rights to your series' distribution? Be sure you understand what types of material you can host on your own website, including embedded players, trailers, or other videos. Exclusive deals may also control your ability to distribute offline as well, including downloads and DVD sales.

Additionally, some hosting sites also work with third party distributors (such as iTunes, Hulu, Roku, and On Demand services). Make sure you know exactly where your show may be headed.

Acquisition fee

Some sites will pay you upfront for your episodes before they are posted online, as a way to reimburse some of your production costs.

Terms can also be negotiated so that you might earn bonus payments if your show performs well and reaches certain thresholds of viewers.

Revenue participation

Many video hosts have pre-roll ads or banners that pop up while a video plays. Some feature advertising elsewhere on their web pages. Others might feature no advertising, but make their content accessible only to paid subscribers. However your distributor monetises their videos, you should negotiate a rate in which you share in the revenue generated by your series. In most cases, this is directly related to the number of views your video receives.

Promotion

Try to get whatever promotional promises your distribution partner makes in writing. Especially if they are the sole exhibitor of your series, you want to make sure that your work has the best potential to be seen. These guarantees can be offered in terms of advertising dollars spent, or in terms of self-promotion, such as the number of days your show will be featured on the site's homepage.

Also, be clear *how* your series can be promoted. Can the distributor cut together their own trailer for your show? Do they need approval from you for any advertisements about the series? Likewise, how can you promote the series on your own?

Ownership

Distributors usually only ask to license the actual episodes (and bonus content, if available) of your series. Check to see if you still retain all other rights to the show. Related and derivative rights allow you to sell merchandise based on the series, for example. They also allow you to produce new episodes outside of this agreement, which would require a new (perhaps more lucrative) agreement in order to distribute. Finally, maintaining copyright of the series concept allows you to possibly adapt the series into another format such as a feature film, television show, or even a graphic novel.

Create buzz without releasing episodes

Sometimes the best opportunities are the ones that you have not even considered. There are many niche-hosting sites that target a specific demographic. These companies may be interested in acquiring your series – and you may have never heard of them before. Likewise, there are always new online portals and networks launching that would like to have exclusive content for their sites.

In order to find these hidden possibilities, web series creators need to increase their show's visibility and raise its profile without distributing any (or, at least, all) of their episodes. Participating in festivals helps this cause, especially if you win any prizes or special recognition. Your first screening at a festival can serve as a free premiere party for your series, too. Also consider sending additional episodes to any members of the press who may be attending the festival. Blog write-ups and reviews are another way to increase your chances of being found by a prospective distributor.

More techniques are covered in a previous chapter regarding the marketing of your series. Simply adapt these methods to be ambiguous about a particular launch date – the classic 'Coming Soon' usually suffices – and encourage fans to follow your series via Facebook, Twitter, or email newsletter. Being able to quantify how much initial interest there is in your show will help inform potential buyers.

Holding onto your episodes for too long could potentially dull interest in your project. For series that required a substantial amount of time and money to produce, however, it is worth your time to find the best possible distribution home. If you feel that you have done your due diligence and could not find the right partnership, then it may be time to explore self-publishing options.

UPLOAD YOURSELF

There are a number of potential hosting sites to post your videos. Each has its own advantages in terms of exposure and promotion, as well as different economic models to help you generate income with your series. If your series is very topical and might feel outdated after a short amount of time, you should certainly distribute yourself as soon as possible.

When searching for the best host for your videos, keep the following points in mind:

Publishing ease

Since you will be uploading several videos at regular intervals, it is helpful if the back-end of the hosting site is as user-friendly as possible. It may be wise to test a system out before committing to launch.

Player quality

Online viewers have little patience for technical malfunctions. If a new viewer stumbles upon your show but is greeted by glitches in the video playback, they probably won't give your project another chance. Make sure that the video and audio quality are at the levels you recorded. Check with friends to see if they have had difficulties with the site in terms of download speeds and video buffering time.

Ways to engage viewers

Look for hosts that not only let users post comments, but sites that give you a comfortable forum to respond. Viewers of your show will become fans if they feel a connection to the creative forces behind the production.

Convenient to share

This medium is all about spreading the word. You want to make it as simple as possible for people to recommend your series to their friends via Facebook, Twitter, Digg, or whatever network they choose. Blogs and video-aggregate sites should also be able to easily embed your videos into their own sites. This will make your work available to users beyond the host's own website.

You can upload to as many different sites as you like, but it is usually easier to focus your marketing strategy on a single platform. Whether you have all of your episodes ready for upload or not, you should create a distribution schedule. This will help your fans find new episodes of your series more easily and create a routine for viewers to watch. To help in this process, most hosting sites let you upload a video and mark as 'private'. Then, you merely have to toggle the video's setting to make it available to the public on your scheduled release date.

YouTube

On the video hosting site that cannot be ignored, YouTube videos receive over three billion views per day.[36] If you want your series to be hosted at a destination with the greatest number of unique visitors, YouTube is the clear choice. Realise, of course, that the site also features the greatest amount of competition, as over 48 hours of video are uploaded to the site every minute.

Still, the potential audience for a YouTube video is tremendous and the view-count numbers for successful channels are simply staggering. Unlike some other hosting sites, though, you are not immediately eligible to receive a share of ad revenue generated by your videos. These deals are reserved for exclusive YouTube partners[37]. You can apply to become a partner after you upload your videos. Applications are judged by content, quality, and number of views. (Like college admissions, YouTube does not offer any explicit requirements.)

Create a YouTube account

The front page of YouTube features a link that allows you to create an account. Try to name your channel the same as your series website URL and Twitter handle, if available.

Upload your videos

Before uploading videos to any hosting site, make sure that you control the rights to all the material involved – this includes music licences, actor releases, and any other copyright clearances[38]. Once the videos are uploaded, under the Standard Licence, YouTube reserves the right to use all or part of your videos for other purposes. Other users, however, cannot use your videos without your consent. You have the option when uploading to select the Creative Commons Attribution Licence, which allows any viewer to use parts or all of your video without needing your consent.

Use your best available resolution to upload; YouTube will automatically make the video available at lower resolutions as well. The player is formatted for 16:9 aspect ratios, but will play 4:3 videos (with solid colour bars on either side). Almost all video formats are supported; project files, images, and audio-only files are not.

Add titles, description and tags

Maintain consistency in the title format for each of your videos. Some producers put the series name in every title, in addition to the episode name and/or number. For the video's description, you can include cast and crew credits, in addition to a summary or tagline. You also have the option of selecting a category that best describes your series. These different categories appear on the left side of most users' YouTube front page and help people sort through videos while browsing for new content. Lastly, add tags that relate your videos to others with a similar theme or that might be watched by the same audience.

Insert annotations and links

Annotations are text boxes that appear over your videos. You can use these to remind viewers to subscribe to your channel, *like* your video, and leave comments. They can also be used to link viewers to other episodes of your series. In the video's description, be sure to include links to your series' website, previous episodes, and social media accounts.

Revenue-sharing platforms

Some video-hosting sites allow advertisements to be played without having to apply for any designated partnership. On Blip, for example, web series producers can select from a variety of ad placement opportunities, or choose to feature their videos ad-free. Break Media also features ads for some of its videos and, like Blip, gives producers the chance to earn revenue.

The video uploading process for these sites is quite similar to YouTube. Producers can create an account and channel for their series. Most sites allow for customisation by adding graphics, playlists, descriptions and credits. Blip also lets users customise the colours and dimensions of the video player, which can be embedded on other sites as well.

Also consider whether or not the site makes view counts public. Online, viewers immediately check a video's total views to help them judge its popularity and legitimacy. If you think your series may be a slow starter, a hidden counter may help you focus viewers' attention on your show's other accolades, such as festival selections and press reviews. On the other hand, if your series is a runaway hit, you want to be able to show off your high numbers.

Additionally, producers can link their web series profile with a PayPal account. Payouts from revenue-sharing platforms usually occur quarterly, with a minimum amount required for a deposit, otherwise the funds are carried over into the next quarter until this threshold is passed. Hosting sites pay their content providers based on a rate called CPM, which stands for cost per mille, or the cost per thousand impressions. That is, how much money will you earn for every 1,000 views your video receives?

Still another option is available to producers who would like to make their videos available using a third-party player and earn ad-generated revenue. Services such as Realgravity and LongTail allow content creators to post videos using their platform technology. Then, producers have the ability to manage ads placed within the video players. Advertisements can be syndicated from premium ad services like SpotXchange or Adap.tv. Ads can also be managed manually, giving you the opportunity to make a direct deal with brands to feature them within your player – with pre-roll videos, pop-up banners, or interactive options.

Lastly, when deciding upon which site to upload your series to, consider how much built-in exposure your show might receive. Blip, for example, compiles staff picks and new additions for inclusion on their front page. Destination sites like Break.com move videos to highlighted sections of their pages according to spikes in popularity. With services that only provide player technology, of course, you will be responsible for driving the majority of traffic to your series.

Non-revenue platforms

There are several other hosting options for users who are not interested in placing advertisements over their videos. Vimeo, for example, is a popular choice because of its player quality and design. The site also highlights some of its most popular videos on the front page, including editorial favourites. The site also offers channel subscriptions, embed ability, and user comments similar to YouTube – as well as more detailed viewer statistics.

Other platforms offer no advertising potential to their content providers, but do give creators the chance to reach a large audience because of the site's popularity. The comedy site Funny or Die attracts a substantial number of users because of its original content, usually featuring well-known actors and actresses. Independent producers can have their videos exposed to this online traffic. Hopefully, users will rate your project well and recommend it to other visitors to the site.

Finally, some hosting sites include advertisements with their videos, but do not share revenue with content producers. Incentives for creators are offered other ways instead. For instance, some of these sites promote original web series heavily on their front page. Others work directly with producers to customise their show's portal (or main channel page) and maximise the interface's potential. Further promotional support is sometimes offered as well. Dailymotion, for example, shares ad revenue generated whenever a video is watched on a third-party web page using its embed player. This incentivises other sites to feature and promote Dailymotion videos over content from other sites.

SUBMIT TO ONLINE NETWORKS

All of the hosting platforms previously listed allow any users to upload videos to their site. There are, however, host sites that rely on an editorial team to hand pick videos submitted by users. Some of these sites have their own players and make non-exclusive deals with producers in order to distribute. Other sites are merely content aggregators, and simply imbed players from other platforms onto their pages.

Non-exclusive networks

The most lucrative distribution deals to make are usually those that give an online host exclusive rights to exhibit your show. This ensures that anyone interested in your project must visit their site in order to watch episodes, and gives the distributor an incentive to promote the series as much as possible. In exchange for exclusivity rights, distributors may also offer upfront acquisition fees in addition to ad-revenue sharing options.

Not all online networks, however, are interested in making exclusivity deals. Instead, sites such as Koldcast.tv make non-exclusive offers to content creators. They generally do not offer acquisition fees, but do provide revenue-sharing and promotional support. Having a partner with a vested interest in marketing your series can certainly help raise its profile.

When evaluating potential deals like these, be sure to note the length of the agreement term. Be aware of your commitment in case an opportunity for exclusive development or distribution comes along. Some sites merely require a few days after written notice to remove your content and terminate the agreement; others may lock you into a deal of several months or years.

Video aggregates

There are many sites – with new ones seeming to launch every day – that comb the web and post content relevant to their users. Most of these sites accept recommendations. If you believe that your series would be of interest to a site's viewers, you should submit links to where your videos are hosted. Some aggregates will embed these third-party players, so you have the potential to earn ad revenue if applicable. Others sites, such as CollegeHumor, will showcase your videos using their own player.

iTunes

Web series can be distributed via Apple's iTunes application, but only as free video podcasts. Instructions can be found on the Apple website. Producers must submit applications for review and, if approved, will be able to offer their series for users to download using iTunes. Fans can also subscribe to your series so that they can automatically download your latest content.

PAY-PER-VIEW MODELS

Asking an online audience to sit through an ad before your video can be a difficult proposition. Asking them to *pay* for content is an even more daunting task. Some web series producers, though, have had success using pay-per-view revenue models. This requires a bit of creative technical logistics, or contracting through a third-party provider.

Producers can embed their videos on password-protected or hidden pages, and make them available only for paying viewers. Michael Ajakwe, creator of the web series *Who...*, uses such a model. Another option would be to sell the videos as downloadable files. In either scenario, it may be possible to watch the show or pirate the material without paying, but, at the end of the day, these pay-per-view models are really used to solicit donations to support your project. Producers have found that the vast majority of viewers will honour the arrangement.

For a more refined approach, there are digital distribution companies that will host videos behind a pay-per-view wall and process credit card transactions. Mostly, these services are only affordable for larger studios and corporations. However, technology is being developed for independent producers, with varying commission-based or monthly service rates.

LIVE STREAMING

The latest web video technology also allows producers to broadcast live – directly from their studio or home. Simply register with a service site – such as Livestream, Ustream, or Stickam – hook up your camera (or use your computer's built-in webcam), create a unique channel, and begin broadcasting. You also have the options of recording the live webcast so that you can post later, in its entirety or edited into abbreviated highlights.

The online network Streamin' Garage, founded by experienced television producer Mike Rotman, offers a variety of programmes that premiere live each week. He uses a piece of hardware called the NewTek TriCaster, which allows him to switch between multiple cameras – essentially a TV production truck packaged into a small computer hard drive. (More information about the creative and technical potential for live internet broadcasts can be found in the interview with Mike Rotman in Chapter 12.)

Some services also allow remote audiences to simultaneously watch the same programme, creating a united virtual audience. Users wishing to join simply sign up for a particular show's start time, then connect to the video online, which plays in synchronisation across all computers. This allows your audience to interact and chat in real time while watching the show. It also gives you the opportunity to have cast and crew members from the project join the experience.

OFFLINE DISTRIBUTION OPTIONS

Projects developed and produced for the web mostly stay distributed online. As with some of the aforementioned pay-per-view and video podcast models, though, producers have offered their shows as file downloads. This was an especially effective model when slow internet speeds were common and streaming technology offered only low-resolution playback. The vast majority of internet users today, however, have no trouble watching high-definition videos online.

Some hosting sites will make their content available to viewers with Apple TV, Google TV, Roku, or Tivo devices, as well as cable On Demand options. These distribution methods are still essentially made over the web, but they allow digital producers to make their projects available to viewers alongside television programming. When choosing where to host your series, look into which other TV-related platforms the company distributes to.

Like their television predecessors, web series are sometimes collected and sold as DVDs. After a successful first-season run, you may consider putting all of your show's episodes onto a DVD and selling it through your website. There are several companies that can professionally duplicate and package these sets, and do-it-yourself supplies are always available. Many producers include additional content such as outtakes, creator commentary, cast interviews or other featurettes (not available anywhere online) as incentives to prospective buyers. Remember to check the terms of any union contracts you may have entered into, as some require additional bonuses be paid for 'traditional' or 'non-digital' distribution methods.

Another way to make the DVD experience different from the online one, if your show's format allows, is to combine episodes so that they play as longer segments. In fact, some web series are created with this re-packaging in mind. The Sony/Crackle project *The Bannen Way* was released online like a traditional web series. Later, it was taken offline, edited together so that it played as a complete feature film, and sold on DVD.

INTERVIEW WITH KENT NICHOLS

Kent Nichols is the co-creator of the long-running series *Ask a Ninja*, which premiered in 2005. Kent is still a producer on the show and is also content partnership manager at the video-hosting site Blip.

Why should a filmmaker consider producing a web series?

The film festival model – of making a film, hoping that it passes the festival gatekeeper, then hoping it passes a distributor's scrutiny – that seems much more luck-based than releasing something on the internet.

So you prefer the distribution options available online, of going directly to the audience and avoiding the middle man?

Absolutely. It's one of the most liberating things – but it's also one of the most terrifying things for a filmmaker. Because, if you put yourself out there, and you don't find an audience, you don't have anyone to blame.

At what point after first releasing *Ask a Ninja* did you realise that you had something?

We were initially trying to do a very complicated animated series, but just could not get it to go. We were trying to do something complex and expensive that was on the same level as machinima animation, which just lets you access your creativity by using video games as your puppets. But we were trying to do that using traditional animation, and we were way out of our depth.

So we thought about what two people could do using the tools that we are experts at. We know digital video and editing. So we took the worldview that we developed for this project and distilled it down to what one ninja's perspective would be. Essentially, we produced a show with the same economics as a machinima show, where it's just editing, creativity and writing.

We were initially excited when 150 people were watching. We posted the video to YouTube and suddenly thousands of people were watching. And we decided we should definitely do more.

How did you sustain the series?

As the series grew, we definitely focused and put more time and work into the production, but we didn't want to mess too much with the formula that was working. The biggest key to success in online series is a consistent release strategy. So you need to figure out a way to honour your commitment to your audience – whether that's once a month or weekly or daily. You need to figure out ways to keep yourself on track.

There are different ways to do this. For narrative content, think about off-narrative videos, like the *Ask a Ninja* format, that are ways to stretch your budget while you are still building your audience up.

You as an artist need to find a thousand fans who will be willing to give you $100 in services, merchandise, whatever, per year to keep your project supported. When content is so freely available everywhere at all times, you can't just have a pure content strategy. You need to find those people that are hardcore fans, and use your content to create those fans. The most valuable fans cannot be found only using one platform strategy. We initially used YouTube to drive people back to our website.

What does Blip do best? What can people do to get the most out of that platform?

We honestly listen and talk to our producers a lot. Everyone on the content operations side has created a show. We've all been in the shoes of someone who is trying to build a business and be successful in online video. So we have a wealth of experience and knowledge there.

We encourage and give producers the tools to create their own website with our embedded players. It's part of our core business to have producers who have strong websites that are vibrant, and have strong communities and fans of our producers. We don't care about driving traffic back to our home domain. We want to help producers drive traffic to their own sites.

Are there any interesting trends that you see with new series being hosted by Blip?

We are starting to see independent creators understand the bubble a little bit better. There is nothing more frustrating than seeing someone create a really great show that's only four or five episodes. It's really hard to find an audience. We're starting to see people start off with 20 episodes, plus additional content. As a narrative filmmaker, you can make that about 120 minutes, which is about what a feature would be. If you do it correctly, you can structure your release strategy over an entire year, build up that audience. You can earn money from ad-supported views, but also figure out a merchandise strategy to get your fans to help support you so that you can get to a season two.

Ramping up for physical production is a drag, no matter if you are doing a short film or a series. It used to be that you would kill yourself in pre-production, you'd kill yourself shooting, you'd kill yourself in post – and then you would pray that an angel would come and write you a cheque and you would become, like, the next Kevin Smith. The new reality is that there is no angel.

You need to add that last step of having to distribute as well. If you're not thinking about distribution while you're writing, while you're in pre-production, then you're shooting yourself in the foot. Most projects are underfunded, they're understaffed, so the only way you can [be sustainable] is to plan.

I think sometimes we, as filmmakers, want to impress people with what we can do. When it comes to communicating characters and relationships, though, it doesn't have to be all that complicated. You can really start paring it down.

What are some effective examples of additional content?

You need to treat your website as the ultimate DVD. It should be the deposit for all of your material. For example, with *Ask a Ninja*, we have a ninja-speed version of everything that we shoot. (A ninja-speed version is an episode that's at 200 per cent speed.) We get tens of thousands of views a month just for ninja-speed [episodes]. And it's zero production work.

[For a craft-building series I am developing] the audience wants to watch her make stuff in real time. So we're going to release on the website the whole 20-minute videos of her doing the crafts. There is zero extra work in that. Your fans that are hardcore will want to explore your series more. So doing a commentary version, doing a live chat event – doing stuff on your site that really pays back to your audience is going to help build that dedication.

10. SUSTAINABILITY

One of the most difficult transitions to make as a creator is turning an initial batch of episodes into a sustainable series. There are many projects that begin with an interesting, innovative, even beautiful release, but struggle to find the means to create follow-up material. Like a television show, web series should be developed with the intention of making as many episodes as possible.

Some shows distribute content continuously, sometimes once a week, others almost daily. Other series produce a handful of episodes that make up one 'season', then gear up for development and production on a Season Two. In either case, finding the commitment and resources to create new content after first production can be as challenging – if not more difficult – than producing the pilot and first episodes.

EVALUATION

Before moving forward with new episodes, it can be very helpful to take a step back and consider how the first round of production went. Be critical in your self-evaluation. Think about what parts of production were most difficult. What surprised you? Take the time to figure out what worked and what did not. With your new season, you have the opportunity to reshape the series so that it highlights the best elements of your first episodes.

Audience feedback and critical reactions

In addition to your own analysis, you should take a look at the feedback and suggestions from viewers. Be discerning, of course. The internet is notorious for having a number of anonymous users that post purely negative comments. On your video-hosting site and Facebook page, though, you may receive some genuine critiques from fans of your series. Ask them follow-up questions to see if they have more specific notes to give. You do not have to take every point into consideration, but understanding how audiences consume your content can inform future development.

It can be difficult sometimes to read critical reviews of your series. Do not take this feedback personally. Objectively try to understand whether or not the objective of your series was successfully communicated to the reviewer. If not, try to figure out why. Entertainment opinions are subjective, of course, and your show simply may not fit into the tastes of a particular critic. Still, it is always important to think about how you can better convey your intentions and point of view to an online audience.

Who are your viewers?

As you look to your audience for feedback, also evaluate what types of viewers have found your show. You may be surprised by who has stumbled upon your show and become a fan. Your work may resonate with an unexpected group of people, so it is always important to learn about your audience and try to include all types of fans in your engagement. Fortunately, the web offers many ways for creators to analyse viewer statistics.

Video host

Most distribution sites offer viewer statistics to their content providers. These breakdowns will show you how many viewers watch episodes each day, and on which sites they are watching. Some users may watch the show directly on your video host's website; others may view on a player embedded on another site. Tracing how your episodes are shared can help you locate and engage fans more directly. You will also be able to see if your marketing strategies are successful in increasing the profile of your show.

Website analytics

Using a service like Google Analytics or tools available through WordPress, you can find out how many users visit your show's website. Most analysis will also indicate how visitors found your site – whether they typed the URL directly, came via search, or were directed by a third-party site. If there are a significant number of people checking out your show because of a link from another website or blog, then you may be able to discover a new demographic of potential fans.

Facebook page

On your show's Facebook page, there is a tab on the left labelled 'Insights' (available for page administrators). This section allows you to see how many fans like and share your updates. It also allows you to see the gender, age and location breakdowns of people who have liked your show's page.

Twitter mentions

Monitor your Twitter account to see whenever your handle is included in a tweet. Bloggers who review your show may post a link to their post. Individuals may want to spread the word to their friends. In all cases, retweet and show your gratitude for the mentions. Also visit any sites that post information about your show or embed a viewer, again with the intent of discovering and engaging new audiences for your series.

Deciding to move forward

As you evaluate the number of views your series has accumulated and the feedback it has received, you should think critically about the show's potential. Is there interest for more episodes? Do you have a solid group of fans that would like to watch new content? Gathering the financing and resources necessary for additional episodes can be made easier if you are able to articulate and quantify audience demand for your series.

If your series isn't initially the runaway hit you hoped for, it doesn't mean that there isn't any potential to grow the project. Preparing for another round of production, though, requires a considerable investment of your time. Take a moment to think about the goals you identified when you first developed the show. Will producing more content help you meet those objectives?

Lessons learned

While making, distributing and marketing your project, you surely learned a lot about the process of creating an original web series. There may be some things that you would have done differently if you had a second chance. Also, there may be some methods you discovered that made the process easier than expected.

Using these new insights, think about how you might approach producing new episodes differently than the first. Can costs be lowered? Can you reduce production time? Or did the show require more resources than you had initially prepared for? Moving forward, you should have a more accurate idea of what exactly you will need to make new episodes than you did when you put together the proposals for the original series. This information will be vital to securing funding and making preparations for the next shoot.

There are two general types of web series production schedules: those that continuously generate and distribute content, and those that produce a group of episodes at a time. The keys to maintaining sustainability for each scenario differ because of these schedules. Whatever your distribution plan, however, successfully producing new episodes to continue your web series will require an economical use of resources and the support of your online audience.

CONTINUOUS PRODUCTION

With the young medium of web series, there are few (if any) industry standards. Episodes are produced at a variety of different lengths and cover every subject matter imaginable. Therefore, audiences welcome innovation; they want to see something new and interesting, with little expectation of what exactly they are in for.

The only exception to this seems to be that viewers prefer web series to be delivered with a defined and consistent distribution schedule. When can they expect the next new video to be posted? Because there are so many competing sources of entertainment online, if a show's episodes debut sporadically, then audiences tend to lose interest.

Any popular YouTube programmer will tell you that the most significant key to their success is the regularity with which they produce content. These creators promise consistent videos and reward their subscribers by posting on time as promised. If you launch a series like this, be sure to clearly announce when new episodes are coming. Then all of your focus should be on maintaining a shooting schedule that allows you to fulfil this promise.

Economy of time and resources

Generating continuous content requires a strict production schedule. Using your first set of episodes as a template, figure out how long it takes you to develop, shoot, edit and post an original video. Work backwards, then, to figure out when you will need to begin this process each week. Even if producing the series is a part-time job, it will take a full-time commitment to make this possible.

Anticipate what resources you will need each week. If you need to borrow any equipment, be sure to secure these reservations well in advance. Create your next videos based upon the schedules of any actors or crew members you will need to collaborate with. Even while you are shooting an episode, you should be in pre-production for the next videos.

Remember that a web series format can change and evolve as it progresses. As you interact with fans and evaluate the show yourself, you may wish to make some creative changes to the concept. Likewise, as you grind through production, you may want to adapt the series so that it can be produced without completely draining you of resources. In order to maintain their distribution schedule, for example, some shows post videos of behind-the-scenes content or talk directly to their viewers about upcoming episodes. Some break up single instalments into two-part episodes.

Another advantage of working in the new media space is that viewers appreciate transparency from their content creators. If you are working on a video that you think your viewers will love, but it is taking longer than expected, post a video update. Audiences respect how much work it takes to produce worthwhile content. As much as they would love to see new videos as soon as possible, most of your subscribers will understand delays in production.

Continuously engaging your audience

Interacting with your viewers is also a full-time commitment and should be a part of the production process as well. YouTube creators have found the most success by responding to as many user comments as possible. Alphacat (whose YouTube channel has been viewed over 100 million times), for example, began building his online audience by addressing every single comment posted below his videos.

Build fan interaction into your production schedule. Regularly responding to viewer posts will encourage viewers to visit your YouTube channel again, and hopefully they will watch more of your videos. Making yourself available as a creator makes viewers feel like they are a part of a community. If someone has taken the time to share their thoughts about your video, they are likely to become stronger fans and supporters of your project.

You can also communicate with your viewers within the videos themselves. Many YouTube creators address comments directly, which expands the conversation to include other viewers as well. Twitter and Facebook comments should be regularly responded to for the same reasons.

PREPARING FOR A SECOND SEASON

Shows that are produced in defined seasons usually shut down production, focus on distribution, and then must start back up again to make new episodes. This will give you time to develop and write new episodes. Take the time to consider outside suggestions and criticism, then move the series in a direction that you feel is most interesting and exciting.

Making the leap into production for a second season is difficult because you once again must go through the pre-production process of finding locations, gathering equipment, and getting your cast and crew together. Often, web series are produced by asking people to work well below their deserved rates. Calling in favours again for the same project can be challenging.

Motivate your collaborators to join your production again by once more creating a fun production experience for everyone. With a round of shooting already under your belts, the next production can go that much more smoothly. Give crew members the opportunity to take on more responsibilities if they wish. Expand roles for your cast. What you lack in monetary incentives you can make up for by helping people improve their skills and build their résumés.

Financing

Whatever methods you used to raise money for the first season of your series can certainly be tried again as you prepare for a second round of episodes. Now that your videos are online, you have more data to showcase for investors. Highlight the number of views, subscribers, Facebook fans and other metrics to show the size and scope of your audience. Also be sure to include press coverage, critical reviews and festival recognitions. All of this new information can be used to show why your show is a worthwhile investment.

Approaching advertisers after your series has launched, however, can be a challenging proposition. Most brands prefer to be involved in the development process so that they can integrate their message into the content. Some shows have found sponsors after initial release, though, primarily by showing how well their series reaches a specific demographic. For projects that have already been produced, there are resources such as PlaceVine that can help facilitate contacts with potential brand partnerships.

As their series build fan bases, many creators have discovered that audiences are willing to support projects with their own donations. Just as a Kickstarter or IndieGoGo campaign can be used to raise initial financing, these same services can be utilised to secure funding for future episodes. Similar to a public broadcasting pledge drive, ask your viewers for their help to create new content. Once people have seen the level of quality programming that you have delivered, they may find it easier to donate to your project.

INTERVIEW WITH WILSON CLEVELAND

Wilson Cleveland is the founder of CJP Digital Media, the multiplatform studio (under PR firm CJP Communications) which develops, produces and promotes new media branded entertainment content. In 2006, Wilson created *The Temp Life* for Spherion. He has since worked with companies such as Hiscox, IKEA and Trident to produce series like *Leap Year*, *Easy to Assemble* (season two), *The Webventures of Justin & Alden*, *Bestsellers* and *Suite 7*. *Leap Year* is debuting a second season of ten, 22-minute episodes sponsored by insurance provider Hiscox and distributed on Hulu. Wilson constantly finds creative ways of using brand integration to produce sustainable content.

What do companies hope to achieve by sponsoring or producing original branded content?

One of the reasons brands partner with CJP Digital is because we're part of a marketing communications firm so we take a different approach to branded entertainment than a pure-play ad or media agency might. Our clients know going in that we create/produce/promote these shows as an extension of social media communications to engage their intended audiences as opposed to replicating their TV ads on the web. There will always be a new product or service that needs promoting and the goal of any branded web series should be to improve or enhance perception of the brand in a way that fosters growth; however, quality stories thematic of a brand's personality have a much longer shelf life than simply placing a brand's products within the content itself, and should therefore be seen as a longer-term investment.

We produced *Suite 7* for the Better Sleep Council as a vehicle for them to speak directly to their audience and the press about the important role proper sleep plays in overall health. It's one thing to publish a list of the common behaviours and situations that keep us from getting a proper night's sleep, but with *Suite 7* we created a series of narratives with characters and stories that audiences were able to relate to as a means of visually illustrating those common behaviours and situations.

For example, my character in the first episode, 'Guest Disservices', is the hotel manager just finishing an overnight shift when he learns he'll need to immediately cover another 12-hour shift without a break. The character's sleep deprivation is what causes him to be such a jerk to the guest checking in, but that's not what the episode is actually about. The 'Captive Audience' episode with Brian Austin Green that Shannen Doherty directed addresses the issues of working yourself to exhaustion but, again, that's not at all what the story is about. The marketing concept was to approach *Suite 7* as an anthology, the onscreen equivalent of a checklist. We set the series in the same hotel room because it was the only logical location where a bed could be both a physical presence and central story focus without feeling out of place.

Is it your experience that most brands like to be a part of the development process or come aboard a web series once it already has a track record online?

Brands typically want series that are made specifically for them because they need to be able to control the message and position the product or service their own way. Occasionally a brand will fund production of a series that has been running long enough to establish a decent audience, but these deals are usually made with the network or platform, not the creators themselves. For example, Fiat recently funded the entire fifth season of My Damn Channel's *Wainy Days*.

How do you balance the challenges of entertaining an audience with delivering the message of the integrated brand?

As a producer, you need to be really candid from the beginning. Chances are, this is the brand's first web series you're producing, so you sometimes need to remind them they are spending money to create their own media property to tell their own story. There is a reason people fast-forward through ads on their DVR: because they can. The sponsor is certainly aware of this, which is likely at least one reason they are investing in creating an entire web show in the first place, but sometimes they need to be reminded. Online, we'll patiently sit through a 15-second pre-roll on Hulu because we know at the other end we'll be rewarded with that episode of our favourite TV show we hate ourselves for missing. With brand-sponsored web shows, if the 'reward' IS the ad, you've just lost your audience.

We produced a series with Horizon Media for Trident Layers® called *The Webventures of Justin & Alden* which has ninjas, vampires, superheroes, time travel and George Washington as a principal character... so we essentially eliminated subtlety and realism right off the bat like any smart, absurdist comedy does. The genius of Sandeep Parikh and Tony Janning's script is that they immediately established a world that's so ridiculous, so funny, that making the gum itself anything less than a main character throughout the series would be more obvious than if we were trying to keep the branding subtle. You can't sneak a product placement in a scene where the first President of the United States is siphoning gas out of a beat-up Nissan like it's no big deal; and that's why the series worked so well.

Lastly – as a web series creator yourself – do you have any advice that you'd like to pass along to anyone thinking about making their own original series?

Ask yourself two questions: 'Why am I making this series?' and 'Who am I making it for?' Most independent creators don't set out wanting to create a series for a brand; instead they make their show and beat themselves up when they can't get a brand to sponsor and recoup the costs. So decide: am I making this for myself and people like me or am I making this for a brand? Make sure, if it's the latter, that you've done your homework on the brand you want to create the show for.

Who is this show FOR? The beauty of creating for the web is that you can produce a series centred around your interests, whereas, on TV, the goal is to make shows as broadly appealing as possible. Find out where your target audience spends time online and get them interested and involved before cameras roll. They may even help with funding.

11. TRADITIONAL MEDIA OPPORTUNITIES

While it is not necessarily the goal of every web series project, some creators are able to make development deals with traditional media companies to turn their concept into a television show (or sometimes a feature film). Adapting a series into a different medium presents unique challenges, because the process involves more than simply imaging the show in a longer format. Engaging a television audience, for example, is different to the unique experience of interacting with fans watching your show online.

Since web series are inherently episodic in nature, most projects that have made the move to traditional media have done so as television series. There are a few examples, of course, where a web series has been developed as a feature film project. This chapter will focus mostly on adapting a web series for traditional television, but many of the techniques can be used if you believe that your show would make a great movie instead.

A web series differs from its TV counterpart in terms of more than just its delivery method[39]. Marketing a television show, for example, tries to compel viewers to tune into a programme at a specific date and time. Web series are 'on demand' in nature, so that viewers can watch whenever they like. Success online is often determined by a large number of cumulative views. On television, ratings are time-slot specific, counting only the audience that watches at a specific time.[40] Being able to embed videos on other sites allows people to find a web series through a variety of different avenues. Television shows, however, play only on a specific network.

Adapting your web series for television will mean more than just expanding the format to last for 30 minutes or an hour, as you will need to think about telling these longer stories across several seasons. Preparing your concept as a TV pitch will require the same preparation that went into the initial development. Simply showing your videos to a network executive may not be enough for them to imagine what your web series would look like in another format.

Producing a television show offers new opportunities in terms of budget, production value and potential audience. If you are interested in exploring these options, consider the steps in this chapter to help you develop your concept for the TV medium and take it to production companies, studios and networks.

UTILISING THE TELEVISION FORMAT

In order for your series to make the jump from web to television, you will need to make a compelling case for how this move will enhance your series concept. There was certainly a reason that you initially produced your project for the web, even if that reason was necessity or convenience – that is, the web offered the most realistic chance for your work to be produced or represented the medium you knew the most about. Now it is time to discover the unique advantages that producing your project for television might offer.

Storytelling

The common practice is for web series episodes to last only a handful of minutes. An eight- or nine-minute run-time seems like an eternity compared to most of the videos online. How can you lengthen these brief blurbs into television's time requirements? Begin by going back to your development process. Think about your show's particular format and how it would be structured as half- or one-hour episodes.

Sketch comedy

One of the most successful formats on the web is perfectly suited for the medium. Comedic sketches are best when they are brief and require little set-up. They are often topical and push the limits of good taste to find their laughs. This is exactly what the internet was built for. A TV sketch show usually contains several such sketches each week. Will your show only be a collection of sketches similar to what you produced online? Will there be any non-sketch elements? Some shows feature stand-up acts, interviews, hidden camera pranks or musical acts alongside the variety of individual sketches.

Situation comedy

Character-driven comedies follow the basic premise of creating unique, flawed, funny characters and putting them in awkward predicaments. Watching them squirm their way out of a sticky situation is all the fun. On television, sitcoms were traditionally shot in front of an audience with a multi-camera set-up. Many comedies today have moved to the single-camera shooting style, but the heart of their storytelling remains the same.

The main character or characters of your comedy surely have the dynamic personalities needed to carry a series, and therefore could sustain a full season of longer episodes. Do your situations have the same stamina? Are the character relationships and world of your series rich enough to generate scenarios with enough complexity to last 30 minutes?

Think about ways to extract more of these situations from your series. Are there secondary characters that can play a more prominent role? Many sitcoms have an ensemble cast and simultaneously follow multiple storylines to fill each half-hour. Are there arenas in your series that could be explored further? For example, could your workplace comedy also go into the domestic lives of the characters?

Serial drama (or soap)

Hour-long television shows that focus on character relationships are known as serialised dramas – a perfect example of which are daytime soap operas. They carry storylines across multiple episodes and their seasons play like an extended film. The conflicts presented in any given week usually come to a conclusion at the end of each episode, but there are usually unresolved elements that continue into the following week.

As you might with a sitcom premise, think about the types of situations that could entangle your characters. However, you are tasked to do more than imagine short vignettes for webisodes. You will need to find scenarios that challenge character relationships several times per hour, and dynamics that can evolve over the course of several seasons.

Strongly consider developing more characters for your series or expanding the prominence of your supporting cast. Serials feature several congruent story arcs per episode. In order to adapt your serialised web drama into a television show, the majority of your development should focus on adding complexity and depth to all of your characters – including possibly creating new ones – so that you have a strong ensemble that can sustain a hundred hours of television.

Procedural

Unlike serials, procedural dramas are self-contained and reach fulfilling conclusions at the end of each episode. The main characters are consistent from week to week, but each new conflict – whether that be a murder to solve or patient to save – is resolved by episode's end.[41] Whomever the main characters of your web series are, they most likely already have the necessary traits to become television leads. Development for the medium, then, should focus on the premise and the types of mysteries being confronted each week.

Will each episode of your series feature only one such mystery? That is, are there enough potential twists and turns in the problem-solving process to last a full hour? If not, consider introducing a second (or possibly third) that can be addressed simultaneously by another team of characters. Try to come up with as many potential stories as possible using your premise. Pitching it as a television series will involve convincing executives that there are enough weekly situations that will last for many seasons, and then showing how your characters will uniquely handle each of these scenarios.

Anthology

An anthology series has new characters facing new situations every episode. These tales are usually connected only through tone, format, or a general premise. The successful YouTube series *BlackBoxTV* is an example of an online anthology. Transforming the online version into a television show, similarly to adapting a procedural, requires that you show there are enough unique scenarios to fill a longer episode and eventually several seasons of episodes.

Current events

Many popular web series involve a set-up in which the host of the programme talks about entertainment or sports news, trending topics online, or showcases various videos from around the web. Digital distribution lets these creators publish their videos almost as soon as the current events they comment on occur. Using description keywords and tags, they are able to catch the attention of users searching for the relevant topic.

Television shows, of course, can also be broadcast quickly – live daily talk shows, for example – and feature commentary on current events. The nature of TV distribution, however, does not allow shows to gather viewers because of increased online traffic surrounding a particular topic. When pitching an opinion show for television, the focus should be on the unique perspective that your concept offers. Having a high number of views is great, but more emphasis should be put on the number of comments left on your pages, for example, as a better indicator of how many users are engaged with your material.

Documentary

The web is also fantastically suited for documentaries. Non-fiction pieces online are not given time constraints, so they can last as long as needed to tell the story. Usually these works are not held to strict distribution schedules, again giving filmmakers enough time to fully develop their work. Educational and journalistic segments on television (for news magazines and such), however, are generally held to stricter running times and must meet specific deadlines in order to make it on air. For documentaries, making the move from the web to TV requires a creator to demonstrate that their same level of content can be delivered on a television series schedule.

Production value

Producing a television show, especially when in conjunction with a major studio or network, provides you with access to more resources than an independent (or even sponsored) web series.[42] When originally developing your series concept, you most likely were constrained by financial limitations and forced to work with whatever locations, equipment and talent you had access to. For TV, you will have a larger budget and bigger team to help bring your vision to life.

When considering how your project can be adapted to television, think of how you can open up the concept beyond your initial production limits. Are there other locations you would like to use? Could the visual effects be sharper? How could a writing and production staff improve what might have been a one-person web show?

GETTING THE MEETING

Making the move from the web to TV will require an advocate for your series either at a television network or studio that regularly produces TV programming. So the important question then becomes: how do you reach out to the television executives that can help bring your vision to life? There are a few different avenues available to web series creators, but the most successful is the tried and true method of *networking*.

Networking is not an acute action; it is a mindset. Always maintain an entrepreneurial spirit. Seek advice from others. There are so many different ways to achieve success in the entertainment industry – across all media – and you can learn about new opportunities simply by listening to the path that others took.

Independently producing and distributing an original web series will inherently put you in contact with a variety of creative and business professionals. Value these relationships. The people that you collaborate with can be great resources to help you with future projects. They also may be able to facilitate connections with industry executives that lead to new opportunities.

Festivals with development deals

A great way to increase the exposure of your project is to enter a film festival that focuses on or allows web series entrants – of which there are an ever-growing number. Recognising that these are great breeding grounds for new talent, many television studios and networks have partnered with web series festivals to find fresh ideas. Some of these companies even offer development or first-look deals to winning filmmakers. The New York Television Festival, for example, now incorporates web series into its independent TV competition and awards development deals with networks like FX, IFC, MTV and Syfy.

Open pitch sessions

Also be on the lookout for production companies soliciting new pitches and material. These used to be completely rare occurrences, reserved only for start-ups looking to get their feet wet in the industry, and almost always unreliable. Recently, however, television studios have mandated that production companies with which they have deals also begin to develop digital content. In turn, these producers are looking to expand their business to include the acquisition and development of web series, as well as establishing relationships with experienced professionals in new media.

Cold calling

The cold call has a long history of use by young filmmakers, and delivers marginal-at-best results. As previously stated, however, traditional production companies are beginning to take notice of new media content creators and, in some cases, actively seek them out. Contacting a producer out of the blue is still an unsure proposition and may still end with a (hopefully polite) 'no, thank you'. Web series creators with a portfolio of online shows, however, may find more productive responses than writers pitching spec pilot scripts.

Many production companies filter unsolicited calls and ask to be contacted only by agents or managers. At the moment, however, there are not many new media representatives. Even at the large agencies, there are few if any agents whose clients work solely in online content. Therefore, the traditional filters may not apply for calls regarding web series development. Online content creators are expected to be entrepreneurs, constantly looking for new opportunities.

In order to select places to call, start by finding shows (online or on television) that you enjoy and that share something in common with your own series – whether that be the style, genre, target demographic, setting or tone. Use that commonality as you reach out to the company behind the work.

Utilising an agent or manager

Representation is best found through other professionals in the new media industry. Collaborate as much as possible with experienced writers, directors and producers. These contacts may have agents or managers themselves, some of whom may be looking to engage new clients. Be aware that agents and managers should never ask for a fee or payment for hire; they only take a commission from work that you accept after signing with them.

Having representation does not by any means guarantee that you will find future work. Putting together projects ultimately is your responsibility. Agents and managers, however, can be tremendously helpful by putting you in contact with potential buyers and other talented clients. They will do whatever they can to set the meetings; it is your job to close the deals.

PITCHING

Your pitch to a television executive should be structured very similarly to the initial proposals you made while developing the project as a web series. Now you have another tool to help facilitate a sale: fully produced videos of your concept. Use these episodes as a launching point for your TV pitch. What elements – specific actors, a unique production style, general tone, etc – from the web series should the executives pay particular attention to? Which elements will help them imagine your pitch as a television show?

Also think about what topics, set-ups or plotlines you would like to use for your TV pilot. Briefly walk the executives through how you imagine the first episode to be. Use applicable clips from your web series to bring this to life. Next, use other episodes of your web series as jumping-off points to demonstrate ideas for several seasons' worth of television.

You have an advantage over other TV projects being pitched because you have essentially tested your concept with audiences. Talk about which episodes and elements viewers commented on the most. Are there any changes you would make from your initial concept based on audience reactions? Most television pilots are not afforded the opportunity of a dry run before being developed by a studio or network.

Finally, before you go into any pitch meeting, be sure to do your research. Find out what past projects the company has produced, and which ones the executive that you are meeting with developed. Try to determine what other projects the company might have in development. If your series resembles any of these, be sure to highlight what makes yours distinctive. Also study the new media marketplace – blogs such as tubefilter.com and deadline.com are great resources – and try to cite recent web series that have successfully been developed for television[43].

DEVELOPMENT DEALS

Hopefully your pitch meetings go fantastically well and you are able to find a company that would like to be in business with you. What kind of development deals are these places looking to make? For the most part, networks are not interested in repurposing web series episodes for on-air broadcast[44]. Instead, development deals based on web projects tend to look like their traditional predecessors.

As the producer of the show, you will work with the creative executives to develop a pilot episode (or a shorter, proof-of-concept version called a pilot presentation). Your participation in the pilot will depend upon your general experience and level of involvement in the series – that is, do you also star in the show or provide other services beyond producing? The studio or network may elect to pay you a licence fee for your idea, then turn over major producing responsibilities to a third party.

For a scripted series, you may be hired to write the pilot script. Your payment will likely be tied to delivery of this script, with a bonus if the pilot goes into production. The writing task may also be handed off to someone with more experience. As with any deal you make regarding your project, be sure to understand precisely your level of involvement and what control you have over the series while it is being developed.

12. INDUSTRY INTERVIEWS

Like many aspects of the entertainment industry, there is no 'right way' to reach the goals of your web series. These interviews will showcase several unique approaches to web series development, production and marketing. As you will see, the paths to success are as varied and creative as the content itself.

INTERVIEW WITH MICHAEL GALLAGHER

Michael Gallagher is a writer, director, producer and occasional host. He is the creative voice behind the hit YouTube channel TotallySketch, which has over 800,000 subscribers and 250 million total views. His sketches often feature interactive elements – in a choose-your-own-adventure style – that encourage viewers to engage with programmes and watch several different videos while on the channel. Additionally, Michael co-founded the leading YouTube production company Maker Studios, which includes over 250 channels and receives half a billion monthly views.

How much time do you spend on TotallySketch? Do you have a regular team that helps you?

I spend, roughly, 168 hours a week on TotallySketch. But, in all seriousness, working on creating YouTube videos is more than just a full-time job... It's a full-time life commitment! When I am not developing, writing, producing, directing, camera operating, transcoding, editing, colour correcting, sound designing, sound mixing or exporting... it's imperative to spend as much time as possible on promoting the content, interacting with fans and viewers, collaborating with other online talent, and updating my brand-tied social media 24/7. To help take on this massive burden, I have been working with Maker Studios, a digital new media studio that I helped co-found. It's a company that provides several key production resources in exchange for a percentage of the revenue.

Is comedy on the web different from other mediums?

Comedy for the web is different because the only person in charge is the creator of the content itself. There are no studio heads or executive producers or red tape that you need to go through to make whatever it is that you want to create. This allows for the range of content (in style, taste, etc) to be drastically different and often times more original (and random) than anything you would ever see traditionally produced, aside from someone as cult crazy as a John Waters. Making comedy for the web allows you to make things that may traditionally be considered much more 'niche' but are able to find a massive audience online.

Has your YouTube channel led to other professional opportunities for you?

Creating TotallySketch has led to some of the most grand and rewarding opportunities I have ever been granted. I have written, directed and produced massive interactive ad campaigns for major brands such as Samsung, Footlocker, Relativity Media, Disney, etc. I have also been able to get face time at some of the major film studios to pitch my ideas and get scripts read, something that was literally impossible for me to accomplish as a mere independent filmmaker. All of those opportunities are a direct result of the success of my YouTube channel.

What advice would you give to someone looking to create their own YouTube channel or web series?

The best advice is to start. Everyone talks about what they 'want' to do. The key thing is to actually DO it. That's what YouTube is all about. Just doing it. (Nike Corp did not pay me to use that phrasing.)

INTERVIEW WITH AL THOMPSON

Al Thompson is an actor, writer, director and producer, as well as the founder and CEO of his own production company, ValDean Entertainment. His sci-fi series *Odessa* won the Syfy 'Imagine Greater' Award at the New York Television Festival and was a finalist in the NBCUniversal Short Cuts competition. Also, his relationship drama *Lenox Avenue* inked a development deal with BET.com.

What do you look for when developing projects?

I usually try to work backwards. I think about what I have access to already or what things I may have come across in the past that may be interesting to me. With *Lenox Avenue*, I knew that I had a supermarket location, a couple of apartments, and office space through various connections. So I thought about how I could implement these locations into a story, into an idea, and into a series. That way, I did not have to find places based on what I wrote that maybe I could not get or were too expensive.

What, for you, makes a project especially good for the web?

I try to think in a minimalist aspect. If I have a series, I usually do not have more than three main characters at the core. Keep the cast amount low. In television, you may have more characters. For the web, try to keep the storylines to a minimum. In the web, sometimes people want to get to the point quickly, but I like to give the audience time to get to know the characters and fall in love with them.

What makes a good character for one of your series?

I think it's about having a nice variety of things people can relate to. In *Lenox Avenue*, we have characters who are going through a range of different things. One guy is in a situation where he is kind of dating someone, but kind of not. And we have another character who has a long-time girlfriend that he is thinking about proposing to. Then we have another character that is all over the place with his dating life. With that set-up, there will be situations that audiences can relate to.

Do you have your audience in mind when developing a new concept?

You need to have some idea of who your audience is or what kind of market you're going to target. On the other hand, I like to keep things open in a sense. For example, I try to keep my scripts colour blind so that the characters can relate to any race.

An interesting thing that I've come across, after putting a trailer for *Lenox Avenue* online, is that I started getting contacted by a ton of soap opera bloggers. That never would have crossed my mind. We forget that soap operas are a dying genre. So where are all these moms and dads who watch soaps going to go? They are a loyal group, and some of them started to gravitate toward my series. That was a unique situation where the audience discovered me. And that's the great thing about being online.

With *Odessa*, we got into a film festival in Boston. The programmers called to ask if they could put *Odessa* in the Children's block. They thought it would be a great piece for their children's block – our lead actress is a little girl. It's not graphic; there's no profanity. But I had never thought of *Odessa* as being a kids' series. So, again, that was an example of a market tapping me on the shoulder and saying that these people might want to check this out over here.

How much do you like to have the talent in your series participate in marketing and engage the audience?

I think it is definitely important, but it is really dependent on how much the actor wants to do. It's not like doing a network show where you have this contract that requires them to promote the work. For me, I'm creating unique character opportunities for actors. I've had actors who want to assist with the marketing. I look at actors, thinking about how invested they are going to be in a project. I think digital content is such a community. So I like actors that like to promote. But, of course, I never want to force actors to promote. It has to be organic, it has to be natural.

Do you look at the online following of actors when casting roles?

As an actor myself, when I'm up for a role, say, with three other guys, what's going to separate us from getting this role? We're all talented, we all look the role. So what separates you? Professionalism, showing up on time, knowing your lines. Being pleasant to work with. And now, as a producer, I ask people what is your Twitter handle? How many followers do you have? How many Facebook friends do you have? I'm not saying that that will totally get you a part, but if it's down to you and one other person, that can be something that sways the deal to your side. If people are supporters and fans of your work, why would I – all things being equal – pass that up?

How do you delegate work after physical production wraps?

I have my producers who are on the project from start to finish. Bringing on a PR person always helps. That's something I learned early on in my career. I think publicists are very important. The right publicists are always extremely tough to find. There are very few publicists who understand the digital community, who are in touch with bloggers and taste-makers. Whether it's that small blogger with two thousand followers on their Tumblr or that person with a hundred thousand, I like to pay attention to all.

Do you find PR people after the show is completed? Do you show them the finished product and try to bring them on board?

Usually, because nine times out of ten, digital PR is not their primary focus. Usually they are PR for companies or films or TV shows or music artists. Especially if this is your initial project, have your package put together to display the quality of your work, the look of it, and also how invested you are in the project. Are you professional? These publicists are going to try to get you an interview, and they want to know that you are going to show up on time and not mess up a relationship that they have established.

What got you into the web series world to begin with? And what do you like about working in the space?

I knew, as an actor, that I also wanted to create content. I wanted to work with my friends, who are all very talented – whether they're a DP, producer, writer or actors that I've been friends with but never worked with. And the only way we're going to work together is if someone creates something.

For me, I didn't want to work on a feature. I didn't want to fundraise and produce for years to tell one story. It's admirable, and a lot of my filmmaker friends do that. But I just didn't have the energy to do that. When I discovered digital series, I found that I could shoot, like, six pages over a weekend. And then get back up and do another six pages the next weekend. I thought that was not only a great training ground for me, but also a great way to slowly build an audience and awareness in the project.

Overall, for me, it was about trying to create opportunities for my friends and myself. Also, I'm a big fan of old school television. The kind of stuff that doesn't exist any more. Shows that I used to beg my parents to let me stay up late to watch. I wanted to create things that don't exist on TV.

Is there any advice that you would like to give to someone who wants to create their own original web series?

Don't try to do everything by yourself. A lot of my friends get frustrated because they try to do it all. But your project will suffer if you're trying to write, you're trying to direct, you're trying to produce it. But whether you're in LA or New York or wherever, there is such a talented community of people for all positions that want to build their résumé, that want to build their reel. Whether you're in California and you reach out to students in the [University of Southern California] Peter Stark [producing] programme. Or whether you hit up AFI and try to find some great DPs who are trying to build their reels. Or you're in New York looking for production people at NYU or Columbia. To me, there is no excuse. There are so many creative people that want to help create great, quality content.

This is a great place to start, to sharpen your skills. Whether you're an up-and-coming writer and you want to write digital content. Whether you're an actor and you don't have anything for your reel. Create content, create opportunities for yourself. You can't just be an actor. Those days are over. I think you have to have knowledge of producing, you're going to need knowledge of scheduling and assistant directing and casting. That makes you stronger.

INTERVIEW WITH NOAH NUER

Noah Nuer is a French filmmaker and co-creator of the comedic web series *Gnome Syndrome*, which was showcased at Comic Con' Paris and made an official selection by the Marseille Web Festival. The series' brief episodes show a world where gnomes help humans with everyday tasks that usually end disastrously for the little creatures.

How have you approached marketing the series? Are there different techniques for growing an audience in France versus internationally?

Dailymotion really liked our series and put some of our episodes on their homepage. I have a feeling that the phenomenon of 'web series' has taken off earlier and on a bigger scale in France than in most other countries (aside from the US). We've had series that have done millions of views even though they were shot in France. Also the main TV channel tried over a year ago to broadcast a series just as a web series. The fact that we have a strong culture of producing unfunded, non-budget short movies might have something to do with it.

What did you find was the best way to raise funds for production?

We financed it ourselves and everyone donated their time. We made sure to find ways to keep our costs down. The majority of people just do it by passion and in the hope of being noticed.

What have you learned from making your series? What might you have done differently?

We went for a series with a lot of special effects. So we ended up doing one episode every other month. It got us noticed because very few series have high production values, intensive special effects, and such an off-the-wall flavour. However, it is exhausting and I wish at times [that we produced] simple [episodes] to get some quantity.

We also went for a series with few recurring characters (except for the gnomes) and I wonder if that hurts us, or is just a different style. Same question with the fact that each episode is self-contained as opposed to being a series where the episodes are part of one big series.

Probably we should have shot half a season's worth of episodes before launching the series. Although you also learn a great deal when you put an episode out there and see the response before you make the next one.

INTERVIEW WITH SCOTT RICE

Scott Rice is a writer/director working in Austin, Texas. In 2007, he created the comedic web series *Script Cops*, which follows a group of police officers making arrests for crimes against screenwriting. The series was picked up for distribution by Sony's Crackle network, and later as branded content for the screenplay software company Final Draft.

From your experience with *Script Cops*, what aspects make a web series appealing to distributors and sponsors?

It is all about advertising and marketing; getting a sponsor's brand out there. Everyone wants to be a part of a hit viral video that everyone talks about and perhaps gets played on national TV. Sponsors also want something that will drive traffic to their website and Facebook page. A good web series is a tool for that. I think sponsors look for web series that are a natural 'fit' for their brand (for example, Final Draft screenwriting software recently re-released my web series, *Script Cops*, which is about screenwriting). They also look for a series that will appeal naturally to their customers.

You write and direct for a lot of different mediums, including commercials, feature films and music videos. What is unique about creating a project for the web?

It actually was a pretty similar process to writing a spec commercial or writing a short film. The trick was coming up with a formula that could be repeated over and over without becoming tiresome. So that was new. The web series I chose to make was less story-driven and more sketch comedy (repetition/variation of a joke), which was new to me. Rather than the gag being a part of the story, the gag became the story. I strove to make all the episodes really short (about a minute) so jokes didn't overstay their welcome.

Lastly, do you have any advice that you would like to pass along to anyone thinking about making their own original web series?

I'm a big advocate of doing at least one episode on spec so that you have a proof of concept to take to distributors and sponsors. That was invaluable in getting *Script Cops* turned into 14 episodes. Being able to show people what it was and assure people that it worked was key.

INTERVIEW WITH BRIAN ROSS

Brian Ross is a New York University graduate who wrote and directed the five-episode web series *Big Country Blues* in 2010. The show won top prize at the Telly Awards for Drama and Music, was an official honoree at the Webby Awards, and previewed at the Cannes Film Festival.

Your series, *Big Country Blues*, incorporates music into the scenes themselves. Were songs written especially for the show? How did you decide where and how to place them into the narrative?

Considering that *Big Country Blues* centres around a country singer and is also set in the Music City (Nashville, Tennessee), we knew it was imperative to find and create high quality and authentically country tracks – to set the tone, ground the series, and establish credibility in the country music world. This was not an easy feat considering that all of the country songs we wanted to include in the series were copyrighted and cost an extraordinary amount of money to license. As a result, we ended up either writing original music or finding indie country artists who were willing to let us use their music gratis.

The majority of diegetic songs that appear in the web series were original songs written by myself or by the star of the series, Jeremy McComb. Jeremy is an established singer/songwriter in Nashville, so he played an integral part in the creation of original music. We also had our composer, Keith Waggoner, and Brooklyn country artist Michaela Anne write original tracks for the most important musical scenes.

Regarding where to place the songs, at least three to five of the songs in the web series actually appeared in the script, so those were no brainers. For the remainder of the music, our process involved stringing out the series, laying in temporary tracks, then finding, composing or recreating similar-style songs to replace those copyrighted songs, yet maintain the tone, style and mood of the original track.

How can music be used to enhance storytelling?

As a fan and performer of music, I'm a big believer in using music to enhance my stories, establish moods and accentuate emotional beats. Placing the perfect song within a scene can actually communicate things that the dialogue and imagery can't. Whether it's building suspense, driving a montage, or just providing the ambiance to a scene, music is an invaluable filmmaking tool.

What was your biggest challenge with scoring the series?

We were very fortunate to have Keith Waggoner, an incredibly talented musician and composer, on board the project to write an original score for *Big Country Blues*. Keith was recommended to me by one of our two music supervisors, as his style seemed like it was in the same wheelhouse as the music in our project. I reached out to Keith and showed him a cut of the web series with the temporary (and copyrighted) score in place. Keith immediately understood what we were trying to achieve. After a series of lengthy conversations to communicate what we wanted for each of the many, many tracks that appear in the series, going back and forth with revisions and notes, we eventually landed a five-episode score that I could not be happier with.

Do you have any advice for filmmakers interested in creating their own web series?

My advice to web series filmmakers is to NEVER short-change yourself or your production because this is 'just a web series'. This is a representation of you and your team's work; it will be available and accessible to millions. Even though the size of the screen may be smaller, this will be seen and thus you should put everything you have into the writing, directing, acting, sound and cinematography of the project. In regards to music, my advice is to avoid using copyrighted music and paying astronomical licensing and publishing fees, as there are much better ways to spend your money. Research unsigned bands and local acts, and reach into your network of peers to find artists who will allow you to use their music for free.

INTERVIEW WITH SUNIIL SADARANGANI

Suniil Sadarangani co-created and starred in the web series *Bollywood to Hollywood* based upon his own experiences moving from India to the US to pursue an entertainment career. The show has been recognised by several international festivals, and both a feature film and television pilot are in development based upon the series' concept.

Did you create *Bollywood to Hollywood* with a specific audience and distribution plan in mind?

In the initial stages of creating *Bollywood to Hollywood* along with my other co-creators – Saba Moor-Doucette, Anil Sadarangani and Jeff Doucette – we hadn't thought about marketing and distribution at all. We just knew we had to get a series like that out on the web and were pretty much working with our gut instincts. [It was] only after the show started getting a life of its own during production that we started moulding the show, keeping the audience and kind of distribution we wanted in mind.

We did a lot of research during production and came to the conclusion that marketing and distribution for the niche genre of *Bollywood to Hollywood* was quite slim, so we decided to make the web series as a platform and stepping stone to bigger media – TV and film. So we created a TV show and feature film franchise [based upon the concept], but with different plots for both formats.

We also have explored mobile phone distribution and are currently in talks with a few mobile phone distribution firms in India and the US. We have set up all the usual social media marketing channels such as Facebook, Twitter, YouTube, etc.

What has the response been to the show in the US versus India and elsewhere? Are your marketing strategies different depending on the region?

The response to *Bollywood to Hollywood* in the US has been overwhelming. We have just started getting the show out to Indian audiences and are totally surprised at the positive response it's getting in India. Elsewhere, such as Europe and the Middle East, it has been well received as well. Since the show has universal appeal and as the title of the show itself garners an immediate reaction, our promotional strategy is pretty much the same everywhere.

And do you have any specific 'if I knew then what I know now' advice that you'd like to pass along to anyone thinking about making their own original web series?

Definitely try and plan out an advanced promotion and marketing campaign, which will definitely help your chances of procuring funding through advertising. Also, the web has a lot of content. Work out alternate ways to be unique and definite. Explore getting your content on mobile phones where there are more chances to work out a money deal between you, the service provider and distributor. Basically blend creative with business (like a feature film project).

INTERVIEW WITH MIKE ROTMAN

Mike Rotman is the founder and CEO of the live internet broadcasting network Streamin' Garage. The channel features several shows about films and music, which are distributed live over the internet and later made available (unedited) online as well.

Where did you get the idea to begin live broadcasts to the web?

I come from a TV background. I wrote for *Politically Incorrect* and a lot of shows that I really enjoyed being on. And I've always dabbled in the web. Since 1999, I've been making web videos. I made one of the first *Blair Witch* spoofs. I made a documentary called *Star Wait* about people waiting in line for *Star Wars*. I put that up on a website, long before YouTube existed – just one of those little postage-sized QuickTime files. And we were getting, like, 250,000 views a week. It was crazy. I did a project that went up on iFilms and eventually Atom. com. So I've always been involved with web video.

Then, when I decided to take a break from TV, I started directing and executive producing *Kevin Pollak's Chat Show*. And I could see how live-switching worked. I'd always wanted to do that, and now it's completely available because of the NewTek TriCaster. That gave me the idea that this was possible.

So I decided to do this thing on my own. I ended up renting a house with a garage, and I said that I could do this really cheap. I converted it myself and thus began Streamin' Garage. We just started creating our own shows, things we'd always wanted to do.

We're very anti-web in terms [of episode length]. These run an hour. Very professional. Appeal to the post-college crowd, that's who we targeted, with smarter content. For the first year or two we just did what we wanted to do. We didn't worry about money. It was just me training people how to use the equipment.

Did you meet any resistance with the long-form, television-style approach?

The thought at first was that people didn't want to watch the long-form. We had a small, but loyal fan base. Every time the show went live, those people called in. We were on Ustream.tv, and those were our big numbers. We're up to five or six million views. And they were always featuring us because most of the content was webcam stuff. We were providing this professional content. [Ustream] loved us, they embraced us. They even started redesigning their site around high-quality material, which at first was just us. [Audiences] still need to get used to longer content, that's where the future is, and that's where we are.

What kind of equipment do you use especially for live streaming?

The NewTek TriCaster essentially is a TV studio the size of a computer. It's a switcher that you hook your cameras up to. When I was an intern working for Leno in the 90s, we had a giant room full of people switching cameras – this is that, in the size of a computer. It records live-to-drive, so there is no editing. When we're done, we take that file and put it up on Blip and YouTube. And it can also distribute live. You just enter the code for Ustream or Justin.tv or live to YouTube now, and you can broadcast live as well as save onto a hard drive. It's amazing.

So, why live?

I mean, with the TriCaster, it's so easy to edit anyway. And I thought while we're doing that, we might as well go live. Then, creatively, there are so many things that we can do live that we can't do [taped]. It lets us really involve the audience. On *Stupid for Movies*, we can do 'Buy, Rent or Burn', which is one of our most interactive segments. People call in or Skype or Facebook or tweet – they name a movie, and our guests quickly say whether they would buy, rent or burn it. We have a new show, *Super Scary Horror Theater*, where people can Skype in and have their tarot cards read by our host, Ms Dementia.

How do you engage viewers who do not watch live?

On Facebook, we'll put up 'Buy, Rent or Burn' posts, let people post questions, and submit fan art that we'll show on the live show. We have a Twitter account as well, but for our show most people use Facebook.

Have fan suggestions influenced the shows?

Sure. We originally had 'Try This at Home' on *Stupid for Movies*. I thought it was a great idea, but we could never get it rolling. We would name a movie, viewers would watch it, and then it would become a round table discussion the next week. But it never really caught on because people didn't want to watch our show for an hour, then go watch another movie for two hours. So that's something we tried, but it just didn't work out.

Besides talk shows, are there other formats that work well live?

Sketches – *Super Scary Horror Theater* is just a different way for us to try sketch comedy, basically. *Stripped Down Live* is a music show. It's a six-camera shoot that's live, never rehearsed. [As director] I was switching live, and I'm very proud of the whole crew on that. They could barely hear me in the headphones. And it's all of us plus the band, and we're literally crammed in this garage. That was probably one of the hardest things I've ever directed, but also one of the things that I'm most proud of. It definitely wouldn't have been as cool if it wasn't live.

How are you able to get your crew together to put shows out on a regular basis?

Well, nobody got paid. It was really learning lessons about how to do all this stuff for everyone. My goal was: if you help me out, I will help you all get jobs. And it was rough, because people can only give up so much time. I had a great crew to come in and help with some of the technical stuff and be there for the shoots. But then, when they leave, I'm the guy doing everything else, 120 hours a week.

It was really tough, but people started to believe in it. They really liked what they were doing. We had fun. Every single person got a job off of *Streamin' Garage*. It is like the ultimate internship. One of our guys runs the TriCaster for Dr Drew's show. I was able to hire some people at my new gig on *X Factor Live*. We've sort of become the expert place to go to. James Cameron had us come in and help with the *Sanctum* premiere. We've done stuff with Ashton Kutcher's company. So I have done what I promised I could.

Have opportunities for live broadcasting online grown recently?

YouTube has been trying live [programming]. When they premiered, we actually moved *Stupid for Movies* to their 8pm premiere spot. But it's still a slow go. If you go to Ustream, it's more professional, but it's a lot of music specials. And you still see a lot of [celebrities] live streaming from the webcam on their computer. So people still haven't grasped the idea that you can [live broadcast] really well, inexpensively.

We're still a little bit ahead of the curve. But there are a lot of opportunities, because we are the experts. When people want to [produce live broadcasts], we definitely do get called. Which is great. It's sort of a second business. That's our way to make money. Not necessarily on our content, but selling our use of the technology.

INTERVIEW WITH JENNI POWELL

Jenni Powell has worked on several web series including *The Guild*, *The Crew* and *The Legend of Neil*. She is a freelance writer for the digital entertainment site Tubefilter, transmedia consultant, and producer of the YouTube anthology series *BlackBoxTV*.

For any web series creator, one of the keys to success is actively interacting with viewers. From the projects you have worked on, what were some of the most effective methods you found to engage your audience?

The number one most effective method to engage your audience is to ACTUALLY ENGAGE YOUR AUDIENCE. That sounds obvious but it's actually ridiculously easy to screw up. Lots of people try to take short cuts by using Twitter/Facebook/Social Networking bots of some kind: audiences see through that so easily and it will instantly turn your audience against you.

You need a human being interacting with other human beings to be true engagement. I think a lot of creators balk at that idea because it seems on the surface as 'extra work'. But it's not extra at all. It's a vital component of what it means to be a creator on the internet. What creators might not consider is that it doesn't always have to be them alone doing the engagement. Encourage your cast and crew to also interact with your show's community. It's a win-win because the audience gets more engagement and it takes some of the work off your plate. And it's a lot of fun to boot!

As a writer for Tubefilter and active member of the new media community, you have watched the industry grow very quickly over a short period of time. What upcoming opportunities or new trends are you most excited about in the web series world?

I'm excited to see what the YouTube Initiative is going to grow into. (YouTube invested over a hundred million dollars in original content, focusing on longer form, higher production values, programming slates, etc.) There have been mixed reactions since the programme was announced, a lot stemming out of fear of change. But I think it needs to be looked at as an opportunity to move forward in whatever way that shakes out to be. Some channels will fail, others will rise, and I'm going to be watching and working every step of the way.

Do you have any specific 'if I knew then what I know now' advice that you'd like to pass along to anyone thinking about making their own original web series?

I actually think I've been insanely lucky when it came to the opportunities I've been given in this burgeoning industry, so I really don't think I'd do anything different. But I can advise on what was the one single thing that really got me to where I am: always put yourself out there. I got my first production job on a web series (on *lonelygirl15*) because I loved the show and was always offering help. And when they needed it, they took me up on it. The same goes for getting to work on *The Guild*: they needed help, I offered, and then I worked my butt off. So, yeah, two things really: put yourself out there, and, when you get there, put in the work. The rest will fall into place.

INTERVIEW WITH MARK GANTT

Mark Gantt is the co-creator and star of the Crackle.com hit series *The Bannen Way*. The project broke viewing records for the site, receiving over 14 million views in its first six weeks online, and has been repackaged as a feature film available on DVD. He has appeared in *The Guild*, *Leap Year* and the MysteryGuitarMan-directed series *Once Upon*. Mark also directed two episodes of the *Suite 7* series.

How have the various web series projects you have worked on effected opportunities for you in both new and traditional media?

Before creating and shooting *The Bannen Way*, I was just another actor in Los Angeles doing the traditional things to get work: acting class, plays, showcases, casting director workshops and postcards. I only had a modicum of success that way and was frustrated waiting for the phone to ring. Deciding to create my own project was less out of a desire to tell stories and more about the willingness to put myself out there in a lead role and see if the audience and industry wanted to watch me. In a way I was thinking, 'I'll do this, and if nobody responds then I'll figure out something to do. I can always direct.' I guess it sounds a little extreme but I honestly was thinking of that. I felt that I never got the shot at the roles I was right for based on my body of work.

Jesse Warren and I worked tirelessly for six months creating the world based on his original screenplay with the title character Neal Bannen. I drove to his house Monday through Friday and we worked for four to seven hours a day. At the time, I was flying to Atlanta once a month to shoot photos for a magazine and auditioning for commercials and just getting by.

We worked hard to create something that would appeal to the 18–34-year-old males and would work on the web. So we knew it had to be sexy and action packed. While in acting class at the Beverly Hills Playhouse, my mentor Milton Katselas was pushing me towards owning the 'Leading Man' casting and helping me to get past my fears and make strong choices. Jesse was in class with me and was on board to help create the character that would allow me to do just that.

It was an amazing journey, from idea to completion, that included some of the toughest challenges I've ever encountered. The result, though, was life changing. It was so gratifying to have a piece of work that I was so proud of have such a great response from so many people. Doing *The Bannen Way* has opened so many doors for me. I continue to develop projects for the web as well as features and TV, and have the opportunity to meet some of the 'gatekeepers' that I only dreamed of meeting. I'm excited to have an amazing team of managers and agents that believe in me and are helping to create more opportunities in every medium. It's a very exciting time right now.

How important is it to engage an online audience? What have you found are the most effective ways to build a fan base for a web series?

I think it's one of the most important things for any digital series. It's also the easiest, since that's where the audience is watching it. We have more opportunities to engage and build an audience with so many social marketing tools available to us. I think the most important thing is to first know who your audience is, find that niche and cater to them. What content and extras do they respond to and how can you extend your story and world beyond the actual episodes?

It's both a blessing and a curse that tools are so readily available for anyone to pick up an HD camera and edit a polished product. There's so much content out there it's tough to get seen and build an audience. I think the most successful shows know this and are catering to their audience and giving them the type of content and added value that they want and are finding ways to get to that audience.

I'm always recommending that people find the blogs, sites and forums that pertain to their genre and start there, connecting with like-minded people and giving them exclusive content. It's work – I won't lie – and it's something I don't think creators are thinking of when they write something and begin to shoot. They aren't thinking how they will get eyeballs. It's a different way of thinking; it's thinking of it as a business and not as an art form. The more you prepare for the launch and distribution before you even put pen to paper, the more this will help to inform what the world looks like and how best to tell the story on different platforms and lend itself to engagement.

Do you have any tips or advice for filmmakers who want to create their own web series?

I'd say, know your audience and look for opportunities to find the best distribution method for your series and do your homework. Look at what's working and what's not. Too many people don't do the work to look at successful actions of those before them. There's so much to gain by seeing what Felicia Day has done with *The Guild* and branding herself. You can't just 'post and pray' that an audience will show up. You can't just say you'll post to Facebook and tweet about it and they will come. Find the stuff that makes you passionate and tell those stories – then find other people that like those stories and share your vision. Stop waiting and create.

INTERVIEW WITH TERENCE GRAY

In 2005, Terence Gray launched the New York Television Festival (NYTVF), which recognises emerging talent and seeks to connect independent television creators with industry partners. As Founder and Executive Director, Terence oversees all of the festival's events and contests, and works to create as many new opportunities for its participants as possible. He has extensive experience in the television industry himself, as a writer and producer for projects on ABC, NBC and ESPN.

How has the New York Television Festival changed with the increasing popularity of web series?

When the festival first began, we were still thinking about television in a traditional, TV box-centric way, and we expected entries to be traditional 22- or 44-minute television pilots. We soon realised that, not only was it prohibitively expensive for people to create that length of work, but networks and studios actually wanted shorter-form content. In order to give executives pilots with an easier-to-digest length and to allow more people to create content, we shortened the length requirement minimum to four minutes.

With the advent of web series and changing the rules to allow shorter pilots, what we saw was a burgeoning market of people creating shorter content that showcased talent above all else – expensive set pieces and special effects mean nothing if it's not rooted in character or strong voices.

What trends have you noticed in the entries?

Of course, we've seen great web series that are incredibly well-produced, shot and edited, but what stands out are the characters and the ability of the creator to tell a story. Also, we have been very pleased to see that creators of web series are able to use the internet to galvanise an audience or a fan base so effectively.

The NYTVF has a fantastic track record of working with major television studios and networks to offer development deals to festival winners. How have you been able to establish these partnerships? What are TV executives hoping to get from the festival?

More than anything, studios and networks want to find talent. Technology has provided awesome advances that allow more artists to create professional-level pieces, but it's yielded an overwhelming amount of content (more than any one executive or development team could realistically sift through). What we provide for networks and studios is a hub of quality content and talented producers. We do this by fostering new talent as well as creating a community of Officially Selected Artists that submit many times over. Through the festival, outreach events, partnerships with other organisations and extension events around the globe – like NYTVF London, which we launched late last year – we have striven to create a network of people that can work and create together.

Additionally, by allowing development partners to specify what they're looking for – for example, unscripted character pieces with A&E or alternative comedy for IFC – we've created a greater efficiency for all parties. We can say to an artist, 'You want to be in business with VH1? Here's what they're looking for.' It's given indie producers additional information and guidance, and allows partners to seek out projects based on their brand.

If a writer/producer's project is fortunate enough to become an official selection, how can they make the most of their festival experience?

The best way to make the most out of the festival is to get in and attend the festival. The festival itself is broken into two distinct categories: our public events (including panels, premiere events and pilot screenings) and what we call NYTVF Connect, which is really the 'business' side of the festival, and what makes the NYTVF unique. Artists can't buy a pass to participate in NYTVF Connect – they have to get in based on the merits of their work.

What is NYTVF Connect?

NYTVF Connect is the festival's comprehensive industry track, serving artists and top-tier entertainment executives across the creative development spectrum and includes exclusive opportunities for Official Artists to pitch, meet and network with the NYTVF's industry partners. This track, combined with our public events (star-studded premieres, Digital and Development Days, screenings of officially selected pilots) really make for a well-rounded and, we hope, useful experience. We want to provide as complete an experience as possible.

Through all of these partnerships and events, what do you hope to accomplish with the festival?

Our main goal is to provide as many opportunities – through both the Independent Pilot Competition and standalone partnered initiatives – for artists to get into the festival, get noticed, and get a deal. We hope that we're viewed as a tangible outlet for creators across the board and that it's not just about the project(s) that got you here, but about the next project you have, the relationships you're building, and the collaborations that can come out of your time with us. Submit, submit, submit – it doesn't matter how you get in, just get in.

INTERVIEW WITH SUSAN MILLER & TINA CESA WARD

In 2011, Susan Miller and Tina Cesa Ward won the Writers Guild of America Award for their series *Anyone But Me*. The show, which began its three-season run in 2008 and has received over 11 million views, follows a group of teenagers dealing with awakening sexuality and identity issues in post-9/11 New York. Susan (*The L Word*, *Thirtysomething*) and Tina (*In Their Absence*) also collaborated on the SFN Group-sponsored web series Bestsellers.

With backgrounds as storytellers in other mediums, what have you liked most about working on the web?

Susan: Freedom. Having an influence. Being at the beginning of something new – risky as that is – where the work isn't driven by the marketplace or inhibited by conventional thinking. Having a voice which can't be diminished by consensus. Making a web series is a powerful way to reach millions by doing it yourself and not waiting for a 'yes' or a 'no' from anyone else. Because you own it.

Tina: Not only do you have freedom creatively, which helps to keep the intention of the story and the point of view of the series firm and intact, you also are your own distributor. You have the choice of where to distribute your series. Of course, that means you have more work, but you're in charge of your own destiny. And I don't see how that's a bad thing for anyone.

Are there types of shows or subject matter that you think work better as web series (as opposed to television shows or feature films, for example)?

Tina: Unlike perhaps popular opinion, I think that there are audiences with varying tastes on the web. I don't think it's strictly one audience or the other. So if you can tell a compelling story, you can bring in an audience. Of course you need to have a very clear picture of who your audience is so that you know where to find them on the web, but there's an audience there for all genres and demographics. Now, I think that series with a niche or minority audience thrive online because, often, that audience is not being served by traditional media. The web is a great place for those that feel like they're stuck on the outside as an audience to find stories about them. And to finally feel included.

Susan: It's limitless. The only rules that apply to a web series are the ones that apply to any creative work. It's got to be original. And compelling. It has to find a way to distinguish itself so it stands out in a crowded field. If a show fulfils a need, it's not about how long it is or what genre it represents. What a series has to offer is the thing that will determine its success on the web or anywhere else.

How have you been able to connect with your audience? (And how cool is it to have an *Anyone But Me* fans' site?)

Tina: If you make an engaging story with honest characters and maintain that strong point of view you had from the onset, you'll connect. We're telling stories that come from our own feelings about relationships and life's challenges; we're just telling them through these characters. And since we're just human beings telling stories that mean something to us, chances are the stories will find others that will have had the same experiences and hardships, and then that connection is made.

Susan: I'd say most of our time outside of production is spent building and holding on to a relationship with our fans. We tweet. We Facebook. We built a website where people can leave comments. We reach out to online media who turn their followers on to us by streaming our episodes. We've been lucky to have a huge niche audience just waiting for a show like ours. *Anyone But Me* is really of our times. We speak to people hungry for stories that reflect their lives. We know who loves us. So we try not to let them down.

Congratulations on three fantastic seasons! Do you have any tips for other web series creators that want to produce (and finance) additional seasons of their own shows?

Susan: Want it. Want it badly. And want to make IT, not a sample of work to get you *other* work. A web series needs time to grow and build momentum. You attract people by making something that shows how much you care about what you're making. So, bring everything you've got and be in it for the long haul. If you want followers, you have to promise them something to follow.

Tina: Multiple seasons are important. Longevity and timing has a lot to do with our success. Building an audience takes time. You have to recognise that and put in the time it takes to get the word out. Financing is always the greatest struggle for any art form. It's just as hard in web series as it is for anything else. I feel we've been talking about financing since the beginning of time and we still don't have an easy answer to it. With a web series, you can look at sponsorship or even product placement to cover some of the costs. Crowd funding has become a big tool. More funding opportunities will certainly start to emerge as the medium grows in recognition.

13. RECOMMENDED WEB SERIES

The ongoing theme of this book has been that there is no 'right' way to create a web series. The paths that shows take to achieve success are as varied as their content. As such, it is helpful to be familiar with as many different web series as possible. Take advice from other creators. Learn from their mistakes. Mimic some of their strategies, or adapt others to fit your own needs.

Listed below are a handful of shows not mentioned previously in the book. Each series provides insight into the business of new media, showcases a unique production style, offers new creative strategies, or is just plain fun. Enjoy!

12 Steps to Recovery – blip.tv/12stepswebseries
Written and directed by Tony Clomax, this soap opera series follows the relationship troubles of a New York actor. Its male, African-American cast and creator have found and engaged an audience that is underserved on traditional television.

Awkward Embraces – awkwardembraces.com
Writer and actress Jessica Mills created a relationship-centric series, featuring the dating misadventures of a self-described 'geek'.

Can't Get Arrested – cantgetarrestedshow.com
Celebrities made famous in other mediums have migrated to the web as a way to flex their creative muscles and make new opportunities

for themselves. Actor Dave Coulier co-created and stars in this series, which also features *Full House* alums Jodie Sweetin and Candace Cameron Bure.

Compulsions – compulsions.tv
Bernie Su created this dark, psychological series and won a 2010 Streamy Award for Best Writing in a Drama.

Dragon Age: Redemption – youtube.com/show/dragonageredemption
Felicia Day, creator and star of the hit web series *The Guild*, worked with BioWare to produce a show set in the world of the company's videogame *Dragon Age II*, distributed by Machinima.com.

Drunk History – funnyordie.com/drunkhistory
Created by Derek Waters and directed by Jeremy Konner, this Funny or Die series features an intoxicated narrator recounting various historical events. The stories are then recreated by a cast featuring Michael Cera, Jack Black, Danny McBride and Will Ferrell.

Pure Pwnage – purepwnage.com
Created by and starring Canadian filmmakers Jarett Cale and Geoff Lapaire, *Pure Pwnage* is a mockumentary series chronicling the awkward social encounters of an aspiring professional gamer. The series went for two seasons online before being adapted into an eight-episode television show on the Showcase network.

Mars and Venus – youtube.com/purplegekomedia
A charming and sharply produced series from the UK about one woman's dating misadventures in London.

Misery Bear – miserybear.com
Chris Hayward and Nat Saunders created a series of sketches for the BBC website starring a mute stuffed animal. Misery Bear also appeared in a video with Kate Moss to raise money for the Comic

Relief charity, and inspired a book titled *Misery Bear's Guide to Love and Heartbreak*.

Those Video Guys – thosevideoguys.posterous.com
British hosts Elisar Cabrera and Sean Harry highlight some of their favourite online videos and interview web series creators on their regular chat programme.

Very Mary-Kate – collegehumor.com/verymarykate
Writer and actress Elaine Carroll stars in the series as a character very loosely based on Mary-Kate Olsen. The show completed its third 15-episode season consisting of videos that are only a minute or two long. *Very Mary-Kate* began as independent productions before being acquired by CollegeHumor.

FEATURED WEB SERIES

All of the web series previously mentioned in this book can be found at the sites below:

Chapter 1: Introduction to Web TV Series
Homestar Runner – homestarrunner.com
lonelygirl15 – lg15.com
Red vs Blue – roosterteeth.com
Smosh – smosh.com
Epic Meal Time – epicmealtime.com
Broad City – broadcitytheshow.com

Chapter 2: Defining Success
Johnny B Homeless – johnnybhomeless.com
Lenox Avenue – lenoxaveseries.com
Odessa – valdeanent.com
freddiew (Freddie Wong) – youtube.com/freddiew
iJustine (Justine Ezarik) – youtube.com/ijustine

The Philip DeFranco Show – youtube.com/sxephil

raywilliamjohnson (Ray William Johnson) – youtube.com/raywilliamjohnson

Totally Sketch – youtube.com/totallysketch

The Fine Brothers Productions – youtube.com/thefinebros

The Guild – watchtheguild.com

Easy to Assemble – easytoassemble.tv

Riese – syfy.com/riese

Mercury Men – mercuryseries.com

Anyone But Me – anyonebutmeseries.com

Rhett & Link – youtube.com/rhettandlink

MysteryGuitarMan – youtube.com/mysteryguitarman

Very Tasteful – youtube.com/verytasteful

The Bannen Way – crackle.com/c/the_bannen_way

Leap Year – leapyear-hiscox.tv

Suite 7 – suite7.tv

Blue Movies – watchbluemovies.com

Elevator – youtube.com/show/elevator

The Morning After – hulu.com/the-morning-after

Burning Love – screen.yahoo.com

The Ropes – crackle.com/c/the_ropes

The Single Life – youtube.com/thedentynegum

Battleground – hulu.com/battleground

Fred (Lucas Cruikshank) – youtube.com/fred

Sanctuary – sanctuaryforall.com

Web Therapy – lstudio.com/web-therapy

Childrens Hospital – adultswim.com/shows/childrens-hospital

The Confession – no longer available via hulu.com

What's Trending – whatstrending.com

StoryCorps: Animated Shorts – storycorps.org/animation

Off Book – pbs.org/arts

A Day in the Life – hulu.com/a-day-in-the-life

GBTV (Glenn Beck) – web.gbtv.com

The Young Turks – theyoungturks.com

Jack in a Box – jackinaboxsite.com

The Burg – theburg.tv
Very Mary-Kate – collegehumor.com/verymarykate
Downsized – downsizedthewebseries.com

Chapter 3: Developing the Idea

L'Altra – martinadego.com
The Apocalypse Diaries – theapocalypsediaries.com
00:24 – twentyfourminutes.com
5 Second Films – 5secondfilms.com
Asylum – asylumseries.com
Ruby Skye, P.I. – rubyskyepi.com
The Specials – the-specials.com
Control TV -- controltv.com
Blood and Bone China – bloodandbonechina.com

Chapter 4: Financing the Project

Pioneer One – pioneerone.tv

Chapter 5: Creating a Marketing Plan

Safety Geeks:SVI – daveandtom.com/safetygeeks
Simon's Cat – simonscat.com
Diggnation – revision3.com/diggnation

Chapter 7: Production

My Bitchy Witchy Paris Vacation – bitchywitchythefilm.com

Chapter 9: Distribution

Who... – ajakwetv.com
Streamin' Garage – streamingarage.com
The Bannen Way – crackle.com/c/the_bannen_way
Ask a Ninja – blip.tv/askaninja

Chapter 10: Sustainability

Alphacat – youtube.com/alphacat

The Temp Life – mydamnchannel.com/thetemplife
Leap Year – hulu.com/leap-year
Easy to Assemble – easytoassembleseries.com
The Webventures of Justin & Alden – youtube.com/thetridenttv
Bestsellers – youtube.com/thebestsellerstv
Suite 7 – youtube.com/show/suite7
Wainy Days – wainydays.com

Chapter 11: Traditional Media Opportunities
BlackBoxTV – blackboxtelevision.com
The Annoying Orange – youtube.com/annoyingorange
Good Night Burbank – goodnightburbank.com

Chapter 12: Industry Interviews
Script Cops – finaldraft.com/products/final-draft/branded-videos.php
Big Country Blues – bigcountryblues.com
Gnome Syndrome – gnomesyndrome.com
Lenox Avenue – lenoxaveseries.com
Odessa – valdeanent.com
Kevin Pollak's Chat Show – kevinpollakschatshow.com
Streamin' Garage – streamingarage.com
Stupid for Movies – youtube.com/user/StreaminGarage
Super Scary Horror Theater – youtube.com/user/StreaminGarage
Stripped Down Live – youtube.com/user/StreaminGarage
The Guild – watchtheguild.com
The Crew – thecrew.tv
The Legend of Neil – effinfunny.com/legend-of-neil
BlackBoxTV – blackboxtelevision.com
Bollywood to Hollywood – bollywoodtohollywood.tv
The Bannen Way – crackle.com/c/the_bannen_way
Once Upon – youtube.com/show/onceupon
TotallySketch – youtube.com/totallysketch

APPENDIX: TWO EPISODES OF ASYLUM SCRIPT

EPISODE 1

INT. HALLWAY - NIGHT

A pair of BLACK SHOES walks quickly down a dark hallway.

BLOOD drips beside each step.

CLOSE ON: A telephone receiver. The bloody hand lifts the phone to the ear of a BEARDED MAN. We only see his mouth, covered in blood, his teeth stained deep red. He speaks with a thick Eastern-European accent.

> BEARDED MAN
> I cannot do this any longer. I cannot work like this.
> > (beat)
> It is not safe. None of us are safe here anymore.
> > (beat)
> No. I cannot leave. She will not let me leave. She will

>   not let any of us out of this
>   place.
>   (beat)
>   I will do what-- Wait. I must go.

The man hangs up the phone. We hear his footsteps echo as he hurries down the hall.

Blood slowly trickles down the receiver and drips onto the floor. Drip... drip... drip--

>   SMASH TO BLACK.

TITLE CARD: "ASYLUM" "Marvin Ulrich: Part 1"

FADE IN:

INT. OBSERVATION WING - DAY

A semi-circle of counters face outward toward glass-walled rooms that line the outside of the observation wing.

DR. SULI URBAN (30s) walks briskly from the hall, flipping through a patient's chart. She'd be stunning if she ever got a good night's sleep.

Trailing Suli is a male nurse, BARTHOLOMEW JACOBS (40s), who's staving off old age with hair gel and highlights.

>   SULI
>   Who's coming here?

BARTHOLOMEW
A deputy director from our very
own Department of Mental Health.

SULI
No, let's do this over the phone.

BARTHOLOMEW
Apparently he's on his way
here in person now.

SULI
Since when did they care about
this hospital?

BARTHOLOMEW
Maybe there's a budget
increase in our future?

SULI
Don't count on it. They'll
keep sending the most
difficult cases in the state
our way. Which I don't mind,
because it means they leave us
alone. Until now, I guess.
          (frustrated; looks around)
Where am I going?

BARTHOLOMEW
You need more sleep, honey.
          (then)
Room Two Seventy-Four. Marvin
Ulrich, age thirty-nine,
transferred in this morning.

Bartholomew nods to one of the rooms, and follows
Suli into-

INT. OBSERVATION ROOM - MARVIN - CONTINUOUS

The small room features only a hospital bed
pressed against the wall. Sitting there is MARVIN
ULRICH (30s), a balding man wearing a short-
sleeve shirt with a tie. When Suli enters, he
immediately hops to his feet and shakes her hand.

                    MARVIN
          Hot damn, it's Kathy Reed. I
          thought we had settled your claim
          yesterday. What's the trouble?

                    SULI
          Mr. Ulrich.

                    MARVIN
          Call me Marvin, ma'am.

                    SULI
          Marvin, I'm afraid you have me
          confused—

Marvin squints at Suli's face, but doesn't miss a
beat.

                    MARVIN
          Of course, Mrs. Cornwell. Has
          my daughter been acting up in
          school again? She's a bit of a
          biter...

Marvin looks at Bartholomew, noticing he's in the
room for the first time, and becomes frightened,
panicky.

> MARVIN (CONT'D)
> Wait. Who's he? You're not
> Mrs. Cornwell. Where am I?

> SULI
> Marvin, it's all right.
> You're at Saint Dympna Mental
> Hospital.

> MARVIN
> I don't remember coming here.
> How did I get here?

> SULI
> We brought you.

> MARVIN
> You kidnapped me. Let me go!

> SULI
> Marvin, please calm down.

Marvin charges Bartholomew and pins him against
the wall.

> SULI (CONT'D)
> Marvin!
> (leans outside the room)
> Security! Security!

Suli flips a RED SWITCH on the wall. An ALARM BELL begins to ring in the background.

Marvin, panting and desperate, hooks his arm around Bartholomew's neck and turns so that both men face Suli.

                    MARVIN
          I don't know who you are or how I
          got here. But I want to go home!

                    SULI
          Marvin, please! I'm a doctor.
          I can help you.

                    MARVIN
          I don't need your help!

Suddenly, the ringing alarm stops--

                    PATRICK (O.S.)
          Yes you do. You need it badly.

Suli turns to find PATRICK AUBERT (30s) - slick and attractive, wearing a cheap suit with an expensive tie - standing in the doorway.

                    SULI
          Who the hell are you?

Patrick ignores her and takes a step toward Marvin.

                    PATRICK
          Marvin, you need to listen to me.

                    MARVIN
          Stay back. I'll kill him.

                    PATRICK
               (holds his hands up)
          I'm not going to hurt you. I
          need you to follow my eyes.
          Look out that window with me.

Patrick points. Slowly, Marvin turns his head to
look.

                    PATRICK (CONT'D)
          Look. It's a nice day outside.
          You've just come back to work
          from your lunch break. You're
          looking out the window in your
          office...

Marvin's breathing starts to calm down as
he stares outside. He releases his grip and
Bartholomew scampers away. After a beat, Marvin
turns to Patrick.

                    MARVIN
          Hello, sir. Are you here for a
          claims adjustment?

                    PATRICK
          I was just leaving, actually.
          Thank you for your help, Mr.
          Ulrich.

                    MARVIN
          Not a problem. Have a good day.

Patrick leads Bartholomew and Suli out of the
room. Off Marvin, looking back out the window—

INT. OBSERVATION WING - DAY

Suli gets in Patrick's face just outside Marvin's
room.

                    SULI
          And what the hell was that?

                    PATRICK
          A simple "thank you" will do.
               (extends a hand)
          Deputy Director Patrick
          Aubert. I'm here to meet with
          Dr. Greenwood.

                    SULI
          He's not taking visitors.
               (shakes Patrick's hand)
          Dr. Suli Urban. I'm running
          this hospital today. Forgive
          me if I seem surprised to see
          someone from the state office
          in person.

                    PATRICK
          It's something new we're
          trying out. I won't make a
          habit of it.

Suli exits down the hall. Patrick follows.

INT. EMPLOYEE LOUNGE - DAY

An employee lounge (possibly a converted nursery)
with large windows on one wall facing the
hallway. There's a coffee maker and microwave,
with a couple of tables and some chairs.

Patrick and Suli stand at one end; Bartholomew
and a young doctor (RACHAEL MENDEZ) are at the
other; an older African-American doctor (TABITHA
LEWIS) sits between them.

                    SULI
          Has everyone taken a look at
          Marvin Ulrich's chart?

                    BARTHOLOMEW
          He came home late from work on
          Tuesday. Drowned his daughter
          in their swimming pool.

                    RACHAEL
          The first thing that comes to
          mind is post-partum psychosis.

                    SULI
          After six years of raising his girl?

                    TABITHA
          Plus it's very rare in men.

                    RACHAEL
          Sure, but only a strong
          condition would drive a man to
          kill his own daughter.

> PATRICK
>
> What if Marvin's current
> symptom's a result of the
> murder?

> RACHAEL
>
> A post-traumatic stress reaction?

> SULI
>
> Marvin hasn't spoken about
> the events of that night at
> all. He could be experiencing
> involuntary conscious memory
> suppression.

> RACHAEL
>
> With no history of mental illness,
> he may have been of sound mind
> when committing the murder.

> TABITHA
>
> That's a chilling thought...

> PATRICK
>
> Let's administer propranolol
> to see if we can steady
> Marvin's mood.

A beat as the other doctors and nurses look to Suli.

> SULI
>
> Thank you for your input,
> Dr. Aubert, but I'll handle
> patient care.

                    PATRICK
         I'm following the department's
         treatment protocol.

                    SULI
         We do things differently here.

                    PATRICK
         And your hospital has the
         lowest discharge rate in
         the country. Your rooms are
         overcrowded and your staff is
         overworked. Maybe you should
         listen to my suggestions.

With all eyes on her, Suli stands her ground.

                    SULI
         I don't like the drug-first
         approach. Rachael's taking the
         lead on this. She'll interview
         Marvin in his current state
         before *anything* is prescribed.
              (holds on Patrick, then)
         It's my call.

Frustrated, Patrick shakes his head and exits.
Off Suli, we split the screen so that our
previous scene plays above and our next one
begins below. This aesthetic will be staple of
our series, and denoted by-- OVERLAP WITH:

EXT. ROOF - NIGHT

TIGHT ON: The end of a cigarette burns. A
familiar Bearded Man takes a drag.

PULL BACK TO REVEAL: Our bearded man is DR.
JOSEPH VASILIEV (60s) and he's joined by Patrick
on the roof of the asylum, a vast expanse of
starry sky in front of them.

>   JOSEPH
>   Saint Dympna has been here
>   since eighteen thirty-two. And
>   yet I doubt that anyone knows
>   what really goes on within
>   these walls.

>   PATRICK
>   Information is hard to come
>   by, I understand. That's why
>   I'll need your help—

>   JOSEPH
>   I have done my part. I took
>   considerable risk just by
>   contacting you.

>   PATRICK
>   What risk? You were attacked
>   by a patient. The greater risk
>   would be not cooperating with
>   me.

>   JOSEPH
>   (shakes his head)
>   You do not understand.

PATRICK
No, I guess I don't. And until
I talk to who's in charge--

JOSEPH
You would like to see Dr.
Greenwood?

Patrick nods. Joseph takes a small NOTEPAD from
his coat, scribbles something, tears the page,
and hands it to Patrick.

JOSEPH (CONT'D)
You did not get this from me.

Joseph flicks away his cigarette and leaves. Off
Patrick, studying the piece of paper, we CUT TO:

INT. HALLWAY - NIGHT

CLOSE ON: The paper in Patrick's hand. It reads:
"613".

Patrick scans the doors as he walks through the
hospital.

Finally, he stops at a pair of doors at the end
of the hall.

Patrick notices someone inside the room and, as
he looks through the window in the door, we go to
his POV--

INT. PATIENT ROOM - TIMOTHY - CONTINUOUS

An expansive, empty space occupied by exposed pipes and thick pillars. In the middle of the room is a small desk and chair. Seated there is DR. TIMOTHY GREENWOOD (30s) - stocky, with a buzz haircut and a strong jawline - holding a PAINTBRUSH with red paint. He wears his white lab coat and an empty gaze.

Suli sits in a chair opposite him. She leans in, speaking softly, more to herself than to Timothy.

> SULI
> I'm sorry I didn't come by
> earlier, honey. It's been a
> busy day.

Suli puts her hand on Timothy's. He does not react.

> SULI (CONT'D)
> I still miss you. But don't
> worry, I promise I can make
> you better.

INT. HALLWAY - CONTINUOUS

Patrick slowly steps away from the window. Off his shocked, confused expression, we--

> SMASH TO BLACK.

END OF EPISODE 1

EPISODE 2

INT. OBSERVATION WING - NIGHT

Patrick and a security guard (LOUIS THURGOOD)
rush across the observation wing toward Marvin's
room.

Rachael sits on the floor, catching her breath.
Patrick crouches down beside her. Louis enters
the patient room.

> PATRICK
>
> Are you okay?

> RACHAEL
>
> As soon as I walked into the
> room, he became hostile...

> PATRICK
>
> Dammit! I knew this was the
> wrong approach!

> RACHAEL
> (still shaken)
> He thought I was a woman named
> Francine and tackled me to the
> floor.

> PATRICK
>
> Before this week, did he have
> any history of violence?

                    RACHAEL
          None. His level of confabulation
          is extraordinary. He didn't
          recognize me at all.

                    PATRICK
          A result of the memory
          suppression?

                    RACHAEL
              (shakes her head)
          He's well past the moment of
          trauma. I think he has some
          kind of amnesia, and his
          memory is so fragmented that
          he has to fill in the blanks
          as he goes along.

                    PATRICK
          But did he begin suffering
          from this illness - whatever
          it is - before or after he
          killed his daughter?

                    RACHAEL
          That I don't know.

Patrick helps Rachael to her feet. Suli approaches.

                    SULI
          What happened?
              (sees Rachael)
          Oh, no.

                         PATRICK
          Are you ready to do things my
          way now? I want ten milligrams
          of Diazepam to calm Marvin
          down. And a hundred-fifty
          milligrams of amitriptyline to
          see if we can get any of his
          memory back.

Rachael looks to Suli; she reluctantly nods.
Patrick hooks an arm around Rachael and guides
her down the hall.

                      PATRICK (CONT'D)
          You need some rest. Where are
          the staff quarters?

As Patrick and Rachael leave, Louis re-enters the
hall from Marvin's room.

                          LOUIS
          Marvin's calm. He was docile
          when I got here.

                          SULI
             (watching Patrick leave)
          Can you get some background
          info on our deputy director?
          Looks like he may be here for
          a while.

Louis nods exits down the hall. Off Suli, we—

                                   SMASH TO BLACK.

TITLE CARD: "ASYLUM" "Marvin Ulrich: Part 2"

FADE IN:

INT. STAFF QUARTERS - NIGHT

A carpeted hallway outside individual staff
rooms. Patrick watches Rachael enter her room and
shut the door behind her.

Then Patrick steps into his own sparsely
decorated, hardwood-floored room and sets a
briefcase on the bed.

As Patrick looks around and allows himself to
take a breath, we OVERLAP WITH:

INT. LOBBY - DAY

An open lobby at the front of the asylum. Suli
sits in a corner with CAMILLE ULRICH (30s) - the
sweet face of this homemaker is betrayed by her
suddenly sunken eyes. Patrick joins them, taking
a seat next to Suli as--

                 CAMILLE
         Over the past week, my
         husband... he became
         unrecognizable.

                 PATRICK
         Did he mention memory loss at
         all?

                    CAMILLE
        No, nothing like that. He was
        so angry all the time. And he
        drank every night. I would
        wake up in the morning to find
        him asleep under the kitchen
        table.

Patrick and Suli exchange looks.

                    SULI
        Mrs. Ulrich, do you know
        anyone named Francine? Marvin
        used that name last night

                    CAMILLE
        She worked with Marvin. She
        had him all torn up. First,
        she beat him out for this
        promotion, then she made these
        accusations - these completely
        made up lies - and she had
        Marvin fired.

                    PATRICK
        That's what started the
        alcoholism?

                    CAMILLE
        He was a very prideful man.
        That hurt him a lot.
            (a beat, then)
        Can I see him?

> PATRICK
> I'm not sure that's--

> SULI
> Your husband... in rare cases,
> alcohol abuse can result in
> Korsakoff's syndrome. Marvin
> is experiencing severe amnesia
> because of this. There's
> a chance he might not even
> recognize you.

> CAMILLE
> He'll recognize me. He'll
> remember who I am. Please.

Camille's eyes are pleading. Off Suli, making up
her mind—-

INT. HALLWAY - DAY

Patrick walks down the hall with Suli.

> PATRICK
> You're completely out of line.

> SULI
> After all this family's been
> through—

> PATRICK
> We don't owe anything to a
> murderer.

                    SULI
        But this woman deserves a
        chance to speak to her husband.

Patrick bites his tongue as they approach—

INT. NURSES' STATION - DAY

Bartholomew sits behind the counter at a nurses'
station in the middle of the hallway.

                  BARTHOLOMEW
        So Marvin really mistook his
        daughter for this Francine
        woman, his boss?

                    SULI
            (nods)
        I think the Korsakoff's was
        that profound.

                  PATRICK
        I assume he's on a Thiamine drip.

                    SULI
        As soon as we suspected
        amnesia.
            (pointed)
        Protocol.

                  PATRICK
        So, his condition won't
        stabilize anytime soon.

>   SULI
> It'll take years of therapy,
> and even then his memory may
> never fully return. When you
> report back, let the Director
> know that our obligation is to
> treat, not to discharge.

Off Suli, her point made—

INT. OBSERVATION ROOM - MARVIN - DAY

Marvin is lying, face-up, with his head at the
foot of the bed. Camille slowly approaches and
leans over him.

>   CAMILLE
>   Marvin?

Quickly, Marvin rolls over and sits on the edge
of the bed.

>   MARVIN
> Samantha? I haven't seen you
> since high school.

Camille holds her husband's eyes for a few beats,
swallowing tears. She speaks slowly, deliberately.

>   CAMILLE
>   No, honey. It's me.

Marvin's expression wipes clean. He looks as if he
may recognize her, and suddenly Marvin becomes sad.

MARVIN

I'm sorry. I'm so sorry.

Camille starts to cry and drops to her knees to hug
her husband. Suli and Patrick watch in surprise.

CAMILLE

It's okay. Everything is going
to be all right.

MARVIN

I swear it was an accident.

CAMILLE

I know. I know. Oh, I've
missed you, honey.

MARVIN

I'm so sorry, Mom.

CAMILLE
(pulls away)
Mom?

MARVIN

It's my fault Rex ran away,
Mom. I left the front door
open. I'm sorry.

CAMILLE

I'm not your mother, Marvin.
I'm not your mother.

Marvin looks at her, confused.

                    CAMILLE (CONT'D)
              I used to be your wife. But
              the man that was my husband
              has disappeared. And he took
              our only daughter with him.

Marvin puts a hand on her shoulder.

                    MARVIN
              Camille, why are you crying?
              What's wrong?

Camille pushes him away, visibly angry now.

                    CAMILLE
              God dammit, she belonged to
              both of us! And you took her
              away. You stole our daughter
              from me!

Suli enters the room. She goes to Camille and
starts to lead her out of the room.

                    SULI
              You should go now, Mrs.
              Ulrich.

                    CAMILLE
              She's gone, Marvin! And I'll
              never get her back!

                    SULI
              Please.

Suli leads her out of the room. Off Marvin,
rocking back and forth, eyes glazed over,
completely lost, we DISSOLVE TO:

INT. NURSES' STATION - DAY

Suli is behind the counter, pouring herself a cup of
coffee. Louis approaches with a manila folder in hand.

> LOUIS
> I checked up on Patrick for
> you.

> SULI
> And?

As Louis shows her the folder, MUSIC UNDERSCORES
and we DISSOLVE TO:

INT. STAFF QUARTERS - PATRICK'S ROOM - DAY

Patrick sits at the end of the bed, reading a
postcard.

> LOUIS (V.O.)
> He's back on the job after a
> two month leave of absence.

> SULI (V.O.)
> What was the occasion?

> LOUIS (V.O.)
> Personal reasons. I'm not sure
> of the circumstances yet.

We flip around to see what Patrick is reading--

Sentences scratched sporadically around the card.
We read, "I know what you need to know." And then,
"I know what has brought you pain." "Find me."

At the bottom, the card is signed with a SYMBOL
- the crude outline of a fish with an oversized X
for an eye.

DISSOLVE TO:

INT. OBSERVATION ROOM - MARVIN - DAY

Marvin moves slowly toward the window. His
jitters calm and his breathing steadies as he
gets lost in the clear sky.

> SULI (V.O.)
> After so much time off, why
> would they send him right back
> into the field?

> LOUIS (V.O.)
> I don't know. I'll keep
> digging.

Off Marvin's blank stare, we DISSOLVE TO:

INT. STAFF QUARTERS - PATRICK'S ROOM - DAY

Patrick flips the postcard over. A painting of
our asylum is on the front. "St. Dympna Mental
Hospital" typed underneath.

                    SULI (V.O.)
          Let me know what else you find
          out. Something doesn't feel
          right about him.

Patrick stands, folds the card into his back pocket,
and heads out. As he closes the door on us, the
MUSIC RAMPS UP and we--

                                        FADE OUT.

                    END OF EPISODE 2

ENDNOTES

1 According to a report from comScore, 1.2 billion people worldwide watched over 200 billion online videos during the month of Octrober 2011.

2 Machinima videos are created in most cases by animators who use footage from videogames and add their own audio track. Web series creator Kent Nichols discusses the medium during the interview in Chapter 12 of this book.

3 Boone, Mike. 'Men gone wild – with food'. The Gazette. 19 January 2011.

4 Rose, Lacey. 'YouTube Sensation EpicMealTime to Become G4 Pilot'. The Hollywood Reporter. 19 December 2011.

5 Zeichner, Naomi. 'The Creators of Broad City Graduate from Improv Class'. The Fader. Aug/Sept 2011 Issue.

6 Angelo, Megan. 'The Sneak-Attack Feminism of Broad City'. The Wall Street Journal. 14 February 2011.

7 Andreeva, Nellie. 'FX Developing TV Version Of Web Series Broad City With Amy Poehler Producing'. Deadline.com. 22 November 2011.

8 In October 2011, YouTube announced the creation of about one hundred channels, each producing original content, through an estimated $100 million investment.

9 It is difficult to determine the rate of unique series upload (as opposed to individual videos), but, to give you an idea, the hosting site Blip.tv, which launched in 2005, currently features over 50,000 unique web shows.

10 This number is also difficult to quantify, but 95% feels like an accurate estimation.

11 Ad revenue varies greatly between distributors and depends upon which kinds of ads you feature: pre-roll commercials before the video starts, pop-up banners during, or post-roll after. (Some sites even allow you to create a 'commercial break' for a mid-roll ad.) To give you an idea of the numbers, videos hosted on Blip.tv that utilise all advertising options earn roughly $1,000 per 200,000 views.

12 A notable exception is the Nickelodeon film Fred: The Movie, based upon the YouTube channel mentioned earlier in this chapter. This adaptation departed significantly from Fred's usual format, though, creating a new story around Lucas's original character. In that respect, the film's development is similar to films like MacGruber or Coneheads that spawned from characters in Saturday Night Live sketches.

13 As a cautionary tale, the sharply produced live web show What's Trending, hosted by Shira Lazar, recently lost its affiliation with CBS News because of an unsubstantiated tweet that proved to be false. Though the message was removed within minutes of being posted, that was plenty of time for the erroneous report to spread across the web and compromise the integrity of the CBS News organisation.

14 As an example, YouTube producers UrbanDictionaryVideo created a series based upon the blog.

15 'Trending' is an increasingly overused term generated by Twitter to denote topics – as indicated by specific hashtags (#occupywallstreet, for example) – that are popular at any given time. Since then, trending has been used to mean any topic that is gaining momentum in popular culture, the media, or news.

16 Some networks prefer shows that are not easily categorised (pay-cable channels, usually). If these networks are your intended buyers, then your concept should, of course, remain decidedly uncategorised.

17 In television, before shooting a full pilot or series, networks will sometimes commission a 'pilot presentation', which is a substantially shorter version of the pilot used to demonstrate the show's potential. Creating a teaser or sizzle reel of your web series to show to a potential buyer is no different.

18 This money could be paid to you, one day. Sponsored web series (sometimes using product integration) are one of the many ways that companies expand the reach of their brands. Understanding the importance of self-branding and protecting the integrity of a series wherever it appears online can help demonstrate to companies that you can create and manage branded content. That can potentially lead to more projects for you in the future.

19 For example, the web series Safety Geeks: SVI was one of the first to distribute a 3D show online. The show's creators are active in the 3D filmmaking community, enter the project into 3D festivals, and promote innovations in the technology. Their show's narrative focuses around the pioneering of 3D production and viewing.

20 The animated web series Simon's Cat provides extra content and message boards for its core fan community of cat owners. Their initial marketing focused on this group of online users, and then expanded over time.

21 A recent trend has been to make a Facebook profile that is inaccessible unless a user 'likes' the page first. This method, however, is just another in the long line of tricks that can be used to inflate viewer numbers – and, in this case, 'likes'. Engage in these practices at your own risk.

22 This includes background actors (extras). Special exceptions may be made under the Taft-Hartley Act, but make sure you contact your union liaison before promising any role to a non-union actor. SAG-eligible actors will need to activate their membership prior to production, which can require certain fees.

23 Down the road, if you wish to make your series available on DVD or have the opportunity to show it on television, your project is subject to the union's Film/Television Agreement. This means that new union minimums of payment come into effect. Make sure you fully understand these obligations before exhibiting your series in any non-digital format that is not covered under the SAG New Media Agreement.

24 In accordance with the local minimum-wage laws.

25 Most American companies require at least a $1 million policy.

26 Your location may require a liability insurance policy, as might the permit agency. A workers' compensation policy will also likely be required in order for you to become a union signatory.

27 Despite what you may read on the internet, it is not a legal practice for a third party to add you as a 'write on' to their policy. It is a waste of money that will not hold up if you ever need to seek protection from the coverage.

28 If you are working with union cast or crew members, the 12-hour workday is mandatory, and you will be asked to submit timesheets for everyone on set. Even if yours is a non-union production, try to maintain this schedule restriction as a professional courtesy to everyone on set.

29 And then send a PA to go pick up. If at all possible, the AD should remain on set at all times.

30 This should be a last-resort method as It relies on the dangerous proclamation: 'We'll fix it in post!'

31 An exception can be made if the change in style is reflected in the story. For example, you may choose to produce a faux-documentary involving the characters from your series. Or perhaps your characters are filming themselves via a personal web cam. Or maybe you would like to produce a fake news report about what is happening in your show. Any such videos can be made with an incredibly different look compared to your other episodes, but should be justified through their own stories.

32 For better material, have a crew member solely in charge of shooting behind-the-scenes coverage. With limited personnel, delegate this responsibility to another producer. You may also have an energetic actor, make-up artist, or PA that loves snapping pictures – feel free to empower this person to roam the set for shots.

33 Online videos come in all variety of lengths, with no direct correlation between run-time and view-count. Realise, though, that viewers can see how long your episode will last before they push 'play'. For many people, seeing a high minute mark – anything above 5 or 6, usually – can be deterrent enough to not even start watching. This is not to say that your episodes cannot be longer, but you will have to overcome a built-in disadvantage if they are.

34 If your composer can record at his or her own studio (or home), then you may be able to negotiate a musician's time for free in exchange for additionally recording a track for one of their own projects. By this stage of the game, you will no doubt be superb at calling in favours and working out alternative methods of payment.

35 'Young' in this sense does not necessarily refer to one's age. It is meant to signify a filmmaker with few credits. Or even someone with extensive expertise in 'traditional' media, but limited new media experience.

36 According to statistics released by the company in February 2011. That number showed nearly a 50% increase from the previous year. Whenever you are reading this book, the number of daily views has surely increased from this initial figure.

37 YouTube also extends its Partner ad revenue sharing to 'one hit wonder' videos. That is, if you post a video that suddenly goes viral and receives a large amount of views, YouTube may reach out to ask if you would like ads (usually banners) to be placed over the video and a share of this revenue.

38 For example, if there is a poster in the background of one of your scenes, you will need to get approval from the artist or printer. (On reality television shows, you may see someone's t-shirt or hat design blurred out for this reason. News programmes are usually exempt.) These types of clearances are often ignored on the web, but be aware that when you agree to YouTube's licensing agreement, you are stating that you unequivocally control all creative rights to your initial video.

39 In fact, since most television shows are also offered online – viewable on computers, tablets, and phones – and many web series can be accessed through a TV with an internet connection, distribution is probably the one element that web and television series have most in common.

40 Ratings are also reported that count viewers who record a programme on their DVR and watch at a later date (some reports add next-day, others include the next seven days). Also keep in mind that TV shows compete against other programmes in a specific time slot. Online, a viewer does not have to choose to watch one video at the expense of being able to watch another.

41 Minor storylines, often pertaining to the domestic lives of a series' professionals, sometimes carry on through multiple episodes. For the most part, though, the idea of a procedural is that the viewer can watch any episode, regardless of its context in the overall series, and effortlessly follow the plotline.

42 In 2009, advertising money spent online surpassed that spent on television in the UK. The US and other countries are not far behind as the amount of money spent for internet ads steadily increases. However, these dollars mostly go to search and banner-type ads, rather than branded video content. The amount of money spent to produce web series remains well below television production costs at the present time.

43 The incredibly popular YouTube series The Annoying Orange is one recent example. An animated series using Orange and the other cast of edible characters was bought by Cartoon Network. Six half-hour episodes were self-financed and produced by the production company The Collective to help make the sale. Again, television executives want to know how a web series with videos lasting only a couple of minutes will look as a 30-minute or hour-long episode.

44 A notable exception is the series Good Night Burbank, created by Hayden Black. Each web series episode has a run-time of approximately 22 minutes, so that it can play (with commercials) during a standard half-hour time slot. The series was purchased for distribution by the Mark Cuban co-owned cable channel HDNet.

INDEX

A

advertising, 13, 21, 63, 69, 76, 78, 122, 128, 166, 170, 192
agents, 24, 91, 156–7, 175
Ajakwe, Michael, 17, 131
AlphaBird, 76
Apple TV, 132
assistant director, 58, 88, 94, 96–7, 101–2
awards, 77–8, 155

B

Beck, Glenn, 28, 186
behind the scenes, 104–5
Blip, 21, 67, 127–8, 133–5, 171, 192
bonus material, 103–4
brand integration, 63, 145
BrandCinema, 63
Brown, Scott, 25

C

camera, 51, 58, 88–98, 101–7, 110, 117, 131, 151, 159, 172, 176
cameras, 11, 29, 80, 119, 132, 147, 171
Canadian, 23, 77, 184
Cartoon Network, 26

cast, 31, 75–6, 83–7, 89–105, 108, 113, 126, 132–3, 151–2, 183–4
casting, 31, 84, 87, 90–1, 162, 164, 175
characters, 33–8, 43–4, 84–5, 151–3, 161–2
CollegeHumor, 120, 130, 185
Comedy Central, 19
composer, 107, 115–16, 167–8
Corddry, Rob, 26
costumes, 84, 93–4, 112
Crackle, 25, 64, 133, 166, 174
creative commons, 116
credits, 61, 64, 72, 75, 86–7, 113, 117, 126–7
crew, 61–2, 73–6, 83–108, 142–3, 172–3
Current TV, 28

D

Dailymotion, 80, 129, 165
Day, Felicia, 23, 176, 184
demographic, 22–3, 63, 71–2, 75–6, 79, 120, 123, 139, 144, 156, 180
Digg, 79, 125
director, 29, 52, 86, 88–9, 94, 96–8, 101, 110

director of photography, 88, 92, 98, 103
documentary, 29, 60, 154, 170
Douglas, Illeana, 23
DVD, 23, 59, 116, 121, 132–3, 136, 174

E
editor, 52, 108, 110–11

F
Facebook, 14, 30, 43, 54–5, 67, 70, 73–4, 123, 125, 138–9, 143–4, 163, 166, 169, 171, 173, 176, 180
Fear Net, 65
featurettes, 22, 105, 133
festivals, 14, 18, 24, 77–8, 119, 123, 155, 169
France, 16–18, 60, 78, 106–7, 165
Funny or Die, 65, 120, 128, 184
FX, 13, 155, 192

G
Gantt, Mark, 25, 174
Gigaom, 75
Google TV, 132
graphics, 20, 70, 72, 74, 84, 109, 112, 117, 127
Green, Seth, 74

H
Hollywood, 19, 168–9, 188, 192
Hulu, 25, 28, 121, 145–6

I
IFC, 25, 155, 178
IndieGoGo, 59, 144
inspiration, 34–5, 53
investment, 15, 20, 58–61, 82, 92, 140, 144–5, 192

iTunes, 79, 115, 121, 130

K
Kickstarter, 59, 67, 144
Koldcast.tv, 130
Kudrow, Lisa, 26

L
lights, 29, 94, 97, 99, 102, 104
Livestream, 131
locations, 21–2, 30, 34, 40, 51, 53–5, 58, 61, 83–5, 89–90, 93–4, 101–2, 107, 113, 143, 154, 161

M
Machinima, 64, 184, 192
make-up artist, 89
manager, 71, 102, 133, 145, 156
merchandise, 13, 15, 23, 122, 134–5
minors, 91–2
MTV, 53, 155
music, 53, 84–5, 105, 109, 112, 114–17, 126, 163, 166–8, 170, 172–3
My Damn Channel, 64, 146
MysteryGuitarMan, 174, 186

N
New York, 13, 19, 28, 31, 66, 77, 90, 106, 155, 161, 164, 167, 177, 179, 183

O
On Demand, 121, 132
one-sheet, 63

P
PBS, 28
pitching, 63, 153, 156
Placevine, 63, 144

401 989

portfolio, 24, 41, 156
premieres, 23, 77, 178
premise, 35–6, 52, 151–3
procedural, 26, 41, 152–3
producer, 14, 16–17, 23–4, 26, 29, 34, 36, 52, 64, 76, 79–80, 86–7, 89, 94–6, 105–6, 115, 131, 133, 146, 156, 158–9, 161–3, 173, 177–8
production assistants, 89
production designer, 89–90, 98
props, 40, 54, 58, 84, 93–4, 96

R
RhettandLink, 24
Roku, 79, 121, 132
Rotman, Mike, 131–2, 170

S
schedule, 12, 30, 54, 58, 65, 81, 85–6, 88, 93–6, 98–102, 104, 107, 110, 125, 141–2, 154
script, 33, 45, 51–3, 83–5, 90, 94, 96, 101, 110, 146, 158, 167
showrunner, 96, 111
Showtime, 26
sketch comedy, 40, 166, 172
soap opera, 54, 162, 183
social media, 63–4, 74, 76, 82, 91, 113, 117, 127, 145, 160, 169
sound designer, 88, 97, 114
special effects, 21, 35, 84, 112, 165, 177
sponsors, 23, 63, 81, 144, 166

Spurlock, Morgan, 28
Stickam, 131
StoryCorps, 27, 186
Sutherland, Keifer, 26
Syfy, 23, 26, 64, 79, 155, 161

T
Thompson, Al, 19, 161
titles, 44, 84, 109, 112–13, 126
Tivo, 132
Tondorf, Woody, 25
transmedia, 16, 43, 74, 173
Tubefilter, 75, 173–4
Twitter, 14, 43, 54, 67, 74, 123, 125–6, 139, 143, 162, 169, 171, 173

U
UK, 16, 53, 55, 60, 184
union, 87, 91, 96, 116, 133
Upright Citizens Brigade, 13
Ustream, 131, 171, 173

V
video blog, 15, 24, 38, 40, 69
Vimeo, 67, 117, 128
Vuguru, 64

W
Warner Premiere, 64
Wong, Freddie, 21, 185

Y
YouTube, 11–14, 17, 20–4, 40, 55, 64, 67, 79, 81, 111, 114, 117, 125–8, 134, 141–3, 153, 159–60, 169–74, 192